When the Beatles hit the c[...] streets, the world changed. C[...] twenty-five women look bac[...] known as the 'swinging six[...], protest and pop, and the first stirrings of the [...] Liberation Movement. Their engagingly personal memoirs describe the sheer fun and excitement of those heady times as well as the euphoria – and the uncertainties – of new freedoms, new struggles. These fascinating pieces, combined with Sara Maitland's perceptive and witty introduction, make *Very Heaven* a wonderful social document.

Sara Maitland, the editor of this collection, was born in 1950 and brought up in Scotland. She graduated from Oxford in 1971 with a degree in English and since then has earned her living as a writer and freelance journalist, publishing widely in magazines, newspapers, feminist journals and fiction collections. Involved in the women's movement since 1970, she has worked with groups such as *Women's Report* and Women's Aid and has played an active part in the Christian feminist movement since 1978. Her first novel, *Daughter of Jerusalem*, won the Somerset Maugham Award in 1979; a collection of short stories, *Telling Tales*, appeared in 1983 and her second novel, *Virgin Territory*, was published in 1984. She is co-editor of *Walking on the Water; Women Talking About Spirituality* (Virago 1983) and was one of the contributors to *Fathers* (Virago 1983). Her more recent publications include *Vesta Tilley* (Virago 1986), *Arky Types* (co-authored with Michelene Wandor, Methuen 1987), and *A Book of Spells* (Michael Joseph 1986). She lives in London and is currently working on a new novel and studying theology.

VERY HEAVEN

Looking Back at the 1960s

Edited by
Sara Maitland

Published by VIRAGO PRESS Limited 1988
20–23 Mandela Street, Camden Town, London NW1 0HQ

British Library Cataloguing in Publication Data
A CIP record for this title is available from the British Library

Typeset by Goodfellow & Egan Ltd, Cambridge
Printed in Great Britain by The Guernsey Press, C.I.

Contents

Acknowledgements

....

For four months in 1968 my parents had five teenage children. I thank my mother for the fact that all of us, including her, survived this.

For four months in 1988 this book has been behind schedule. I thank Ruthie Petrie, my editor, for the fact that I have survived this. I hope she will too, because her steady intelligence and support have added admiration and gratitude to the affection and friendship which I have enjoyed for many years.

I want to thank all my contributors (*sine qua non*) – for their work and additionally for their willingness to expose their younger selves in the photographs – all of which show us as we were then, rather than the superior creatures we have since become.

Also Meta Zimmeck, Mandy Merck, Stephen Sheedy, and Andreos Adamides, all of whom in various ways have helped me enormously.

And finally I would like to thank Frances Molloy and Virago Press for permission to reprint Chapter 7 of *No Mate for the Magpie* and U.A. Fanthorpe and Peterloo Poets for permission to reprint 'At Aversham' and 'Chaplaincy Fell Walk' from *Voices Off* (1984).

A Chronology of a
Decade

Lots of people get muddled about the sixties. I discuss this in more detail in my introduction, but just to orient or remind you, here is a list of the dates of some of the major events of the sixties. You can play an amusing game with it, if you don't mind fights, because everyone will disagree about what happened when and where, or you can use it while reading the book to see how the different lives and different events described mesh with each other – for example, several women mention the impact of the student revolution from quite different angles: by referring to this chronology you may get a sense of their lives meeting and parting as they do. It cannot be a complete list of everything that ever happened between January 1960 and December 1969. Instead the events are simply presented in years in an attempt to give the feel of the variety and complexity of the decade – and to acknowledge how much I have been obliged to leave out. Some of the dates are approximate because some events have specific dates and others last a very long time and have no clear beginning and ending (for example, 'The Profumo

Affair' actually lasted from the summer of 1961 when John Profumo first met Christine Keeler in Stephen Ward's swimming pool until the Macmillan government fell in 1964). Beyond the decade, the American military involvement in Vietnam began in 1954 and continued until 1972.

1960

Harold Macmillan, on tour in Africa, makes his 'Wind of Change' speech

First of the thalidomide victims born. The births of babies injured by the drug thalidomide peaked in the first half of 1961

Sharpeville Massacre in South Africa

The Divided Self by R.D. Laing published

Cuba nationalises 70,000 acres of US-owned sugar plantations and establishes full diplomatic relations with USSR

The L-Shaped Room by Lynne Reid Banks published

1961

J.F. Kennedy becomes President of the USA

Penguin Books prosecuted under obscenity laws, and found not guilty, for the publication of *Lady Chatterley's Lover* by D.H. Lawrence

Cuba defeats US invasion at the Bay of Pigs

South Africa leaves the Commonwealth

Suicide is decriminalised

1962

First session of the Second Vatican Council called by Pope John XXIII

Marilyn Monroe dies

E. Lubbock, Liberal, elected at Orpington by-election

Harlem Globetrotters' first British tour

First transatlantic live television broadcast shown in UK

Cuban Missile Crisis

The Golden Notebook by Doris Lessing published

1963

J.F. Kennedy shot

First Beatles single released

Silent Spring by Rachel Carson published

Buchanan report on *Traffic in Towns* published

The Spy Who Came In From The Cold by John Le Carré
published

Bob Dylan issues 'A hard rain's a-gonna fall'

The Great Train Robbery

First 'children's demonstration' in Montgomery, Alabama,
USA

The Profumo scandal surfaces

Honest to God by John Robinson, Bishop of Woolwich,
published

Hugh Gaitskell, leader of the Labour Party, dies

Up the Junction by Nell Dunn published

A Summer Bird-Cage by Margaret Drabble (her first novel)
published

1964

The Labour Party wins the General Election and Harold
Wilson becomes Prime Minister

The 'Mods and Rockers' riots and violence at UK seaside
resorts such as Brighton

Darling starring Julie Christie released

Nelson Mandela imprisoned

1965

Sir Winston Churchill dies

Capital punishment abolished

Mary Quant opens Bazaar

Rhodesia declares UDI

1966

The Maharishi visits the UK for the first time

Gwynfor Evans, Plaid Cymru, elected to Parliament as the
first Welsh Nationalist MP

Ian Brady and Myra Hindley convicted of the Moors
Murders

England wins the World Cup against West Germany in soccer

1967

Winifred Ewing, Scottish Nationalist, elected to Parliament

The Naked Ape by Desmond Morris published

Homosexual acts, between consenting adults in private, decriminalised
The *Torrey Canyon*, oil freighter, wrecked off Cornwall
The Arab/Israeli Six Day War
'Sgt Pepper's Lonely Hearts Club Band' by the Beatles released
Abortion law reform
Release (organisation for drug and other legal rights) founded by Caroline Coon

1968
Martin Luther King assassinated
Robert Kennedy assassinated
Les événements in Paris
Humanae Vitae, Pope Paul VI's pronouncement that birth control methods other than the Rhythm Method are 'contrary to natural law', and therefore unacceptable to Roman Catholics, promulgated
Tariq Ali becomes president of the Oxford Students' Union
Soviet Union invades Czechoslovakia
Chicago Riots, led by The Weathermen, at the Democratic Convention
Student rebellion starts at Warwick University
Grosvenor Square demonstrations against the Vietnam war

1969
Woodstock rock festival in up-state New York
Richard Nixon becomes President of the USA
No-fault divorce, proven only by 'the irretrievable breakdown of relationship', legalised
British troops are mobilised in Northern Ireland
First moon landing
Salvador Allende elected President of Chile

Sara Maitland

'I Believe in Yesterday' –

An Introduction

On 6 August 1962 Marilyn Monroe died of an overdose of barbiturates in her Hollywood home.

On 4 October 1970 Janis Joplin died of an overdose of heroin in her Los Angeles hotel.

Abstractions (what is left when you have sucked out, abstracted, the particular and personal detail and left only the general or symbolic content) – of eras, of cities, of virtues and vices – are nearly always female in Western culture, so I do not apologise for seeing in both of them personifications of the fifties and sixties. In Monroe's case the symbolism is more straightforward – it was a more straightforward decade. Less than three months before her death she had flown to Washington to sing 'Happy Birthday to you' to that male symbol of regeneration and hope, President Kennedy, holding court in Camelot; it was a pretty tacky occasion by contemporary standards. Less than a year after she died, he did too. Neither fifties femininity nor old style personality politics proved sustainable. But nor did the alternative: by the time hippiedom came to its most public flourish, at Woodstock, in 1969, Janis Joplin – its symbolic female presence – was so stoned that she was scarcely able to perform; she was also seriously considering a 'retreat' to small-town Texas and marriage. Somewhere between these two deaths a 'terrible beauty was born': the Women's Liberation Movement. Though as we have since learned, and ought to have known already, it was a very long pregnancy!

The points of similarity between the two are easily stretched. Both came from small-town middle America. They both died from addiction to the fashionable drug of their time; they had both started taking their poison because they believed it would help them work. Both their careers were in decline, and both died believing that they were about to experience a come-back. Both of them were depressed about their emotional 'failures'. They both died alone. They were both women. They were both not merely great Stars, but also almost mythological representations of the decades that made them stars.

What is more fascinating is the ways in which Monroe and Joplin were entirely different. Just to look at in the first place. And the second place. But also in the manner of their performance: Monroe projected perfection and innocence and did it through the mediation of the camera – and she acted 'parts' which, however much they were designed as vehicles for the star herself, still made a passing pretence at being acting. Joplin was a live performer, and her attraction was precisely the loss of perfection, the absence of innocence and the presentation of her 'self' – however much this self was in fact a part. Monroe was romantic, Joplin raunchy.

In less than ten years what was seen to be desirable in a woman had radically changed. Robyn Archer and Diana Simmonds in their book *A Star is Torn*[1] argue that the change was only in style, in media presentation; that the similarities between them, springing out of the tensions inevitable to women who want to be successful, overreach the differences, and the common pattern of femaleness runs on unbroken. I am not convinced.

The fifties are perceived from where we are now as the decade of femininity, the seventies as the decade of women. What happened in the ten years in between that changed that? During that decade, while I was growing up, something was happening that produced in 1970, not only Joplin's death, but also the first British National Women's Liberation Conference, at Oxford. Understanding what happened is extremely important to me; feminism does seem to me, as Sue O'Sullivan says, to be 'my life' and in that sense, born in 1950, I am the person who I am because of the sixties. Looking at my own writing, particularly my fiction, I find in it increasingly both an exaltation of and a lament for the sixties. Something very extraordinary happened to the world then, and particularly to women, from which we have mercifully not fully recovered and with luck and the more measurable qualities of endurance, analysis and hard work may never do so.

My daughter and her friends, all born in the early seventies, laugh at the sixties: their laughter was the starting point of this book. I responded to it by an earnest and intense desire to explain. But in fairness I felt that I had to give them a space to express that ridicule. What I found, though, was that they were not alone; there is a great deal of ambivalence in many of the writers in this book. With hindsight we do sort of know that the so-called Sexual Revolution did in many ways 'rip us off'; that we were not as happy as we wanted to be, and that throwing off the shackles of parental approval left us open and vulnerable to peer group pressures in ways that were not always healthy. A few of the writers here go further and actually denounce the sixties as a negative experience and one best forgotten as soon as possible, but I cannot agree with them. Angela Carter rightly points out:

> There is a tendency to underplay, even to devalue completely, the experience of the 1960s, especially for women, but towards the end of that decade there was a brief period of public philosophical awareness that occurs only very occasionally in human history; when, truly, it felt like Year One, when all that was holy was in the process of being profaned, and we were attempting to grapple with the real relations between human beings . . . furthermore, at a very unpretentious level, we were truly asking ourselves questions about the nature of reality. Most of us may not have come up with very startling answers and some of us scared ourselves good and proper and retreated into cul-de-sacs of infantile mysticism: false prophets, loonies and charlatans freely roamed the streets. But even so I can date to that time and to that sense of heightened awareness of the society around me in the summer of 1968 my own questioning of the nature of my reality as a woman. How that social fiction of my 'femininity' was created and palmed off on me as the real thing.[2]

Yes, yes, I want to say and am surprised at how strongly I endorse her statement, particularly as, for almost all of the 1960s, I was not part of what was happening; and on the whole was not enjoying it at all. But interestingly practically every woman I have spoken to while working on this book, from Julie Christie (the *Darling* Girl, the symbol of all my yearning adolescent hopes) onwards, also felt that the sixties were really happening just over there where people were younger, older, more 'cool', more turned on, having more fun, or simply better at it. The sixties started for me in January 1962 when, after years of excited anticipation, based on a desire to be like my brothers, I was shipped off to my girls' boarding school and discovered within twenty-four hours that it was a hell-hole – an opinion from which I never wavered in six whole horrendous years. They ended equally depressingly in an NHS mental hospital, whence I was released in December 1969. (The seventies, and not only by comparison, were wonderful and suited me much better.)

Retrospectively there were at least three good reasons why the sixties were at first inaccessible to me: class, geography, and physical malfunction. To take the last first: I was – as I still am – tone-deaf. In any other decade this would almost certainly have proved a minor inconvenience, a cause of mild pity and considerable exasperation in my friends (as in fact it does now); but music was central, crucial I believe, especially in the early sixties, to creating and communicating a mood and meaning among people of my age. Far more than books, or even fashion, music was the marker, the expression of what we wanted. I could indeed observe that Paul was cute and John clever and Mick Jagger sexy, but so were lots of young men. Indeed at the time when it was a human necessity to have a favourite Beatle I chose Ringo mainly because he was the only one I could be sure of accurately identifying since his nose was large and the drums just couldn't be confused with a guitar. The important thing about this tone-deafness was that it cut me off not just from the music itself, but also more immediately from my own peer group whose enthusiasm – even in a girls' boarding school – was real and binding. Teenagers, as Patricia Vereker points out here, for the first time, perhaps as a response to the new advertising being directed at them, were defining themselves against their families within the support of a tight peer group identity; the bonding glue of that group identity was the music: the songs, the bands – or groups as they were quickly called – and the fashions they generated. This was obviously more powerful in some settings than in others, but even in its mild and adult-controlled form within the closed world of my school I was an outsider and could not disguise it.

Superficially more serious were my defects of class and geography, which were tightly linked. I spent my school terms in a small town in Wiltshire, as successfully immured from the big bad world as the system could manage; nothing could pass the *cordon sanitaire* without permission, and this included books. (They circulated of course, including four or five loose pages of *Lady Chatterley*, a strange *samizdat* text, much crumpled from being shoved under or into things at the approach of grown-ups: I didn't read the whole novel until I was at university and by then it was too late for me and Lawrence to get together.) From 1964 moreover I spent my holidays in rural south-west Scotland, mainly in the company of my family. Our social life, at least until we could drive, was entirely controlled by adults: mine favoured the dinner jacket (or kilt) and long dress sort of entertaining for evening, and the wellington and anorak events for day time over anything that I would have considered 'cool', if I had the capacity to calculate it.

It is interesting that nonetheless I knew what I was missing. In 1966 I scandalised my youngest brother's prep school by winning the sisters' race in a very short cotton dress (or so they thought; I look at the photographs and wonder what all the fuss was about) which I had made myself. I was proud of it, but knew even then it was the limit of what I could get away with, not what I really wanted. I cannot read pieces like Marsha Rowe's and Alexandra Pringle's without a deep sigh of envy: it was not until after I had left school that I ever entered the portals of Biba. Instead a travelling dress-maker (Polish and into yoga) stayed at our house and sewed my very pretty pale blue silk coming-out dress which I wore with a wide tartan sash and my dead grandmother's pearls. I was not very good at those country parties; my heart was not in it, but I was baffled about the alternatives. I had already sensed that at exactly the time I was ready to take advantage of the privileges of birth and wealth their joys had departed: neither upper-class accents nor High Tory political training were passports to the world I dreamed of entering. I wanted something different, and I knew it was out there. Books I hadn't read, drugs I didn't know the names of, clothes I couldn't wear, and ideas I didn't know how to think. The best I could do by way of protest was to learn to smoke, write poems that did not rhyme, and to be thoroughly obnoxious – with grief at home but glee at school – and wait; or, as Michelene Wandor puts it in her poem, yearn.

The flip side of all this was that I did know, at least at an emotional level, partly because of class privilege itself, about the politics and happenings of the big world: it was my parents' world. In 1962 I learned about the Cuban missile crisis, very personally, because one of my parents' closest friends was an Admiral in the US navy. He was staying with us, we took a lovely sunny day-trip to Cambridge, and as we walked along the Backs, US Embassy personnel were searching for him personally; he had to fly home that evening to Defend His Country against the dangers of communism. The following year I knew about the Profumo affair too, rather lopsidedly, because it was bringing down the government. My father, to my mother's annoyance, taught me a bitter little limerick about it, which he encouraged me to recite to his Butlerite Conservative friends and which accurately reflected his politics:

There was a young girl called Christine,
Who shattered the Party machine;
It isn't too rude
To lie in the nude,
But to lie in the House is obscene.

(And I must say it says something about the bankruptcy of parliamentary democracy in this country now that people then really expected the entire government to fall simply because a member of it had lied in the House of Commons about his personal life – I could not but remember this during the Belgrano incident. None of us really thought that the government would not get away with lying.) From 1964 I certainly remember exactly where I was when I heard that President John Kennedy – whose handsome young face hung on many an adolescent teenage wardrobe door along with the Beatles' – had been shot (half way up a flight of stairs in my school: I could pin-point the step if I could bear to go back inside the building). A little later on I did know about the supposedly depraved sexual goings-on of the Rolling Stones and Marianne Faithfull because the father of a school friend of mine was the judge at their trial. I cannot now remember what who was supposed to have done with a Mars Bar, but I

7

do know that under our respectable and daughterly shock we were all immensely excited by our tenuous contact with such an excitingly wicked world. In the summer of 1967 my brother and I drove to Edinburgh to see Marianne Faithfull star in Shakespeare's *The Winters Tale* and the combination of that serene blonde beauty and what we knew about her was itself a culture shock – people like that were allowed to be in Shakespeare!

In 1968 things looked up a bit; my place at Oxford assured, I was sent off to the USA on my own for seven months. It ought to have been a time to break out, but although my skirts were spectacularly shorter than anyone else's – hippies and counter-culture and the politics of protest and feminism may all have been US imports, but the mini-skirt was truly British – and my class accent not so readily identifiable, I wasn't really up to it. It was six months of being the wrong person in the wrong place at the wrong time, just. I left Washington the day before Martin Luther King was shot, and arrived in Los Angeles a week after Robert Kennedy's assassination. In San Francisco I did go to Haight-Ashbury, that Mecca of free love, drugs and counter-culture, but I went as a tourist. From that perspective it seemed sordid and scary, and I left at once.

I arrived in Oxford in the autumn of '68, more virginal in more ways than now seems credible. I don't remember feeling any connection whatsoever with the hippies and their drugs, mysticism and music; or with the politicos and their Parisian excitements, though Tariq Ali was head of the students' union and I went (again like a tourist) to hear him speak; or with the 'sexual revolutionaries' who whizzed off to glamorous London and complained about the repressive college which expected us to be in bed, alone, by eleven o'clock. I coped pretty well with the shock of discovering that I was not the cleverest person in the whole world, but failed entirely to find a way into the very real and active intellectual storms that were brewing here and there in Oxford – Marxist literary groups, and structuralist seminars. I knew it was going on and I wanted it and I just did not know how not to be an outsider.

And then, just in time, in 1969 I stumbled into a new group

of people; they were Americans and they were, like most sane Americans of a draftable age, Against the Vietnam War – they were draft avoiding mostly, though some of them had burned their cards and were heroes. They were bright, nice, middle-class boys, most of them Rhodes Scholars, and several of them now both eminent and respectable. But then they hung out in a shambolic house in North Oxford with a roneo machine, a medium amount of dope and a considerable loneliness fused with a great solidarity with each other: civil rights and the draft had converted all of them into politicos – and the roneo was there to duplicate their newsletter for European draft resisters. What they gave me was a connection point between politics and personal lives, the abundant energy that comes from self-interested righteousness, a sense that there were causes and things that could be done about them, and large dollops of collective affection. (A year later they were to give me, rather unexpectedly, an introduction to something more important: the women's movement, although I do not recall that before one of them took me to hear Germaine Greer preach at Ruskin College in January 1970 we had ever mentioned the subject. But I certainly would not have found it so soon, so redemptively and so happily without that connection.) I owe them an enormous debt and, if it were not for a sad, sneaking feeling that some of them would be embarrassed by it now, I would name them here.

My world was transformed. The sky was bright with colour. I smoked my first joint, lost my virginity and went on my first political demonstration. I stopped attending lectures and my ears unblocked so I could actually hear what was going on around me. I realised that classical education, Whig history and compassionate liberalism were not the only values in the world. I was in a constant state of excitement. Too much happened too fast really and as I said at the beginning I ended the sixties in a mental hospital, whose brutality and repression completed my emotional-political education. But I want to make clear my total conviction that it was not my abrupt absorption into this new world that drove me into a quite genuine nervous collapse, but a complete clash of values. It was the miseries and repressions of the preceding ten years. I collapsed from a sudden surfeit of joy. Even then I knew it. I emerged from the hospital into the seventies with no doubts at all about where I now belonged. Things change, of course, but I have never looked back.

And I am still greedy to know how it happened. How did we move from the fifties' passive model of femininity, epitomised in Marilyn Monroe, to the feminism of the seventies? What was happening to so many of us that made that extraordinary explosion of politics and personal lives possible, indeed obvious, in the early seventies? What was the impulse that shook the lives of all the women who have contributed to this book – women with well over forty years' difference in age, with origins in five continents? Why did the mood of that decade have such wide-ranging effects that five of the women left the country of their birth and never went home again; that a happy teenager from a tight-knit Welsh mining community came to London and still sees her two illegitimate children as a triumphant liberation (Joan Fletcher); that a respectable teacher at Cheltenham Ladies' College threw it all in to write poetry and live with her woman friend (U.A. Fanthorpe). I am unashamedly and greedily curious, and I think I ought to be.

Now I look at my own fiction and find, over and over again, a pride in the sixties, a regret which is not nostalgia for a golden youth, but a conviction that we badly messed up an historical moment which had been constructed out of lives that will not be lived again. A period that was culturally significant, an explosion of energy. I wrote once, in a fictional persona:

It is still so hard for us middle-aged, middle-class lefties, left over from the bright sixties and the promise of Paris. We know with a well concealed bitterness that if by some amazing chance our youthful hopes are ever fulfilled we will not fully enjoy it having now entered into too much of the old kingdom and exchanged our squats for mortgages. I spend about a third of my life envying my less principled – or puritanical – contemporaries their success and another third deploring my own. The third third I spend not thinking about it because it is all too sad saying farewell to all the brave promises, and driving people around London at all hours to expiate my guilt at being able to afford a car – albeit a seven-year-old Renault 6, carefully chosen to lack all possibility of chic, radical or otherwise.[3]

As the times get harder and it seems increasingly difficult even to manage decent strategies of resistance, let alone any truly creative political intervention against Thatcherism and the social injustices which are daily escalating, it seems to me more and more that I, at least, have to understand the sixties better, explore that terrain more carefully for signs both of hope and of self-criticism. That is why I wanted to edit this book.

I wanted to edit it, rather than write it, because one of the most important things of the time was the liberating of individual voices into defining collective experience. It was in part that valuing of the collective over and above private ownership, which even in its silliest forms was an insistent part of the sixties, which made the women's movement and the other radical political activities of the seventies possible. It is the wearing away of that commitment which makes the materialism and the devil-take-the-hindmost political philosophy of the eighties possible.

In preparing the book I have been looking for a balance between those who 'created' the sixties culture and those who 'consumed' it, on the assumption that there is a symbiotic relationship between the two; and that both are of equal importance. There have been four specific difficulties, all of them interesting, in finding the right material, the right women. The first I mentioned at the beginning of this piece; the conviction that wherever you were and whatever you were doing, the 'real' sixties were somewhere else; probably on a different continent, or at least in a different country, different city, different street, different psyche. I am increasingly convinced that this is partly because the protest against the fifties took such extraordinarily diverse forms that no one could be participating in them all; particularly as the sense of

11

internationalism increased radically through the decade. It was also partly because much of the brou-ha-ha of the sixties was, at another level, a media invention, so it was impossible to be there. Moreover women who engaged with the seventies and absorbed the message of collectivity also learned that there was no such thing as individual leadership, or authority; and thus it is impossible to believe that you as an individual at that individual time were actually important. I believe that this is morally and analytically correct, but it has been a great bore for me as editor trying to convince people that they have something to say about what happened there.

The second difficulty is also small but fascinating. A surprising number of women, while happy to admit that the sixties in some general sense were important to them, seem to suffer from an odd amnesia, or at least chronological confusion. They cannot date events, even major public ones: they cannot 're-member' the decade in any objective way. For instance, while quite a lot of people can remember the specific personal details of hearing about Kennedy's assassination, I sat at dinner with eight women of about the right age, both American and British, and we could not come up with an agreed date – not even a universally acceptable year, never mind month. The chronology is hopelessly blurred. It would be too easy to suggest that this was because we had all been consuming excessive quantities of mind-destroying drugs: people seem infinitely clearer about both the fifties and the seventies. But curiously even drug-free, reactionary historians of the decade seem to have the same problem: Bernard Levin published *The Pendulum Years* in 1972, but although he goes into inordinate details about all sorts of events, it is a history book almost entirely lacking in specific dates. I have become so fascinated by this phenomenon that at one point I considered publishing this book with an accompanying 'kairology' – listing for major events all the dates I had been offered in the course of my researches, without confirming or invalidating them. I decided that this was not entirely helpful, and you will see that I have offered at least a partial chronology, although it is subjective and selective, to help readers, and myself, through this problem.

Another difficulty was a surprising sort of embarrassment from many people about their own moral seriousness at the time: a kind of flippancy or even shame that they should have cared so much, believed so strongly, and engaged so fully. Clearly we were entirely wrong in a belief that if we smoked enough dope and screwed enough people the world would be transformed, the revolution brought in, and Eden replanted, but the fact is – whatever she says now – re-reading *The Female Ennuch* it is clear that Germaine Greer did not go around without her knickers on for hedonistic delight alone, nor did the *Oz* editorial people publish pictures of Rupert Bear with his cock out for pornographic motives. Libertarianism was of course fun (at least for a great number of women), but part of the fun was the conviction that it was brave, important and socially useful, liberating at a global level, to do these things. It says something about the cynicism of the eighties that so many women feel deeply apologetic about their own ethical enthusiasm. Or perhaps the embarrassment is the other way around: a guilt that we have, collectively and individually, retreated from such high hopes. There is a not fully conscious realisation that a generation which thought itself, politically and culturally, so radical was able to indulge in those aspirations precisely because of the success of capitalism. The sixties were born out of the 'you've never had it so good' years. The security provided by the relatively high employment and rising wages of all classes, the expansion of education, particularly tertiary education, the technological advances (the first moon landing – which just made it into the sixties – was the mythological symbol of these advances, but they were experienced daily in, for example, cheap flights, live international television and the real reduction in the necessary hours of housework), all created a new dynamic in society: a youth group which was both monied and leisured compared to any previous generation. This of course does not deny that there were devastating injustices, prejudices and real poverty. But the present knowledge that we, as a social group growing up after the war, have come to prefer personal affluence and influence over moral seriousness when a choice was forced upon us, makes it very tempting to deny the reality and passion of moral aspiration; to feel cynical and embarrassed by those younger selves. Certainly more comfortable than feeling cynical and embarrassed by our present selves.

A final, and telling, difficulty for me as editor, is the now-amazing absence of women from so many of these events. I really had forgotten: forgotten the sneers when Barbara Castle was made Minister of Transport; forgotten the fact that a prosecution lawyer could really ask a jury if *Lady Chatterley's Lover* was a book they wanted read by their 'wives and servants'; forgotten that major international events could take place with the total absence of women, not merely physically but even psychically. One event, central to the mood of the sixties, and which probably affected directly and indirectly more women's lives in the world than any other single incident in the decade is not even mentioned in this book – the Second Vatican Council. It is not mentioned because no British women were there; only one woman – an American nun – was invited to contribute to this massive international forum, which met for over four years; and until late in the decade no one even articulated a complaint against this fact. Women's absence, both actual and perceived, from so much of what was going on may indeed explain why women have difficulty remembering the events, and insist that they weren't really 'where it was at'.

And yet we were not absent; we were there, we were participating and we were learning: and if it was not 'very' heaven for most of us it was at least something of a 'peak in Darien' (to exploit another romantic poet as mercilessly). Far from silent, but with 'wild surmise' we stood there and saw the infinite possibility of a huge new world – a vast ocean waiting for our exploration. With Angela Carter I believe that this was an historic moment and therefore worthy of record. Much as Sue O'Sullivan, among other contributors, may feel awkward about being turned into history I continue to believe, following Sheila Rowbotham, that recording our lives, seeking our pasts, is an important activity.

> The writing of our history is not just an individual gesture but a continuing social communication. Our history streng-

14

thens us in the present by connecting us to the lives of countless women. Threads and strands of long-lost experience weave into the present. In rediscovering the dimensions of female social existence . . . we are uncovering and articulating a cultural sense of what it is to be a woman in a world defined by men. We are tracing the boundaries of oppression and the perpetual assertion of self against their confines. We are heaving ourselves into history, clumsy with the newness of creation, stubborn and persistent in pursuit of our lost selves, fortunate to be living in such transforming times.[4]

The sixties were transforming times, the beginning of the transforming time for almost all women in Britain. Many, although not all, of the contributors here would identify themselves now as feminists; practically none of them do so remembering their younger selves. But since there are now women around claiming to be 'post-feminist' I have no qualms whatever in identifying these writers' lives as 'pre-feminist' in an important way. We were undeniably greedy, both for personal experience and for instant transformation, undeniably arrogant in our conviction that we could indeed summon up the 'very heaven' of my title simply by being young enough, energetic enough and bloody-minded enough. Nonetheless the predominant feeling that comes to me from these articles is not one of greed and arrogance, but of optimism and excitement and aspiration that must be worth recapturing, even if we have to do it without the naïvety of last time.

Notes
1. R. Archer and D. Simmonds, *A Star is Torn* (Virago 1986).
2. Angela Carter in *Gender and Writing*, Edited by Michelene Wandor (Pandora 1985).
3. Sara Maitland, 'The Eighth Planet' in *A Book of Spells* (Michael Joseph 1986).
4. Sheila Rowbotham, *Dreams and Dilemmas* (Virago 1983).

GROWING

....

'We were so much younger then . . .'

Moureen Nolan and
Roma Singleton

Mini-Renaissance

It wasn't easy, even in Liverpool, trying to adapt to the swinging sixties in a Catholic convent grammar school. My first realisation that the impact of the Beatles ran deep was when our uniform was altered and a trendy lapel-less blazer (first sported by the Beatles on Granada's 'Scene at Six Thirty') and a skull cap (currently sported by Pope John XXIII) were featured amongst the bottle green one-inch-below-the-knee skirt, socks and regulation knickers.

I've often thought how schools of that kind naturally attracted teachers who were oddities and eccentrics; people in whose hands my formative years were being shaped and moulded. And as Lady Lillian, our ancient maths mistress, perched high upon her pedestal desk, smoking 'Passing Clouds', and loftily proclaimed that diamonds should never be worn before noon, the minds of the students before her were fixed on the lunchtime escape to the Cavern. Busy chrysalises elbowed each other in the toilets, abandoning and adapting tell-tale evidence of high school morality, rolling skirts at the waistband to within a whisper of indecency, the more dextrous skilfully dabbing long 'bambi' lashes on upper lids and short, thick lower lashes under lower lids. Then, pansticked and panda-eyed, the transformation complete, we swarmed down Mount Pleasant, aware that we were at the hub of something exciting and new. Young people suddenly had an important voice; they were being listened to, followed even, and Liverpool youth was at the front of this heady cultural thrust. It didn't matter any more that my scouse accent was raw and unrefined, there were people all over the country envying and trying to imitate the guttural tones that singled me out as a Liverpudlian.

In a very short space of time, names like the Beatles, the Merseybeats, Gerry and the Pacemakers, Tommy Quigley and Cilla Black became overnight successes, monopolised the Top Ten and charged popular music with a very distinctive sound. The upshot of this was that any and every teenager who could tap his foot in rhythm had thrown open his front parlour window, gathered three mates together, signed an HP agreement with Frank Hessy's music store, and was rocking away with the requisite set of drums, amp, rhythm and bass guitars.

I suppose the excitement stemmed from the belief that anything was possible, it was all within reach. Something to do with this magical starmaker quality of being Liverpudlian. I remember going to Butlin's in Filey in 1966 and it was natural for people to assume that if you didn't actually know a Beatle, at least you knew *someone* famous. As it happened I did. Billy Kinsley (formerly of the Merseybeats, and after of Liverpool

Express) only lived across the road in Fedora Street and came into our sweet shop regularly. Freddie Starr was a one-time visitor to my brother's late night practice-cum-poker sessions, and struck me as an oddball even then.

And I was luckier than most Beatle fans because a fellow member of 3X was one Sheila Phillips who lived in Forthlin Road, the same street as Paul McCartney. Of course we made her take us round.

Disappointingly, Sheila seemed to grow more nervous and forgetful of house numbers as we, Maureen McGuinness and I, were busily working ourselves up into a state of typical adulating fan-semi-hysteria. Imagine, actually being on the same road that he'd been in, standing looking down the path that he'd walked down so often, gazing at his front door; even better, peering through his letter-box. Sheila, steadily paling, said, 'Don't, you can't go peeping through the letter-box.' She put her hand across it, while Mo peered through a gap.

At that moment, inevitably, the door was yanked open. A middle-aged lady appeared, rightly indignant. Bearing in mind that this was certainly not the first time she'd been peeped at by complete strangers, she didn't appear to be as annoyed as she might. It was poor Sheila who now, because of her attempts to get us to desist the apparent ring-leader, took the brunt of the lady's complaints. She tried to protest her innocence. We took care to stand behind her, peeping out from each shoulder, gently shaking our heads, tutting and glancing our disapproval at each other. Having done this much to ally ourselves to the lady we, with growing confidence, asked a barrage of questions about our hero. When was he due back? Later on, she told us, and gave us to understand it would be *much* later on. What was he having for his tea? What was his favourite tea? Bacon and eggs to both of those. In retrospect I can say that she, his aunt or house-keeper, must have been a very patient and long-suffering woman. But patience ran out and we were asked to move on. We did. All of twenty feet away. We reasoned that if she was cooking his tea, then he had to be coming home reasonably soon.

As we waited Sheila, torn between genuine upset at the

injustice and a desire to see Paul, moaned gently about what her mum would <u>say</u> when she discovered that she had been caught peeping into neighbours' houses. Just then – a diversion. That looked to be a familiar face coming along the other side of the street. Yes – Terry Sylvester of the Escorts. We shot over to him – he'd do while we were waiting. The Escorts were a fairly well-known group at the time, and I suppose it says something about mid-sixties Liverpool that this could happen in an ordinary residential area – while waiting for one superstar to arrive we should by chance meet this other quite famous group member who lived just round the corner.

We abandoned him however when a dark green Jaguar saloon pulled into the road and stopped outside Paul's house. We weren't even amazed that George Harrison was driving and that Paul stepped out. I think we gave a cursory scream – well that's what you did – and then between the questions told him that he was having bacon and eggs for his tea. He too was polite and patient and spent five or ten minutes talking, signed autographs and left. It is a measure of how accessible to people in Liverpool the Beatles seemed to be that I didn't treat the autographs like the crown jewels. That ownership of the Beatles by Liverpudlians was I think responsible later for a kind of scouse resentment, as though we should all have shared in their material success. We had produced all these chart topping groups, why were the rest of us all still skint?

But the term 'superstar', which today equates with demi-god status, had not been invented: if they were superstars, and those that did survive undoubtedly are, they came quite cheap, packaged even. All-star concerts meant just that – Dave Dee, Dozy, Beaky, Mick and Titch, the Walker Brothers and the Bee Gees all in one show for thirty shillings. It may have been to do with the proliferation of groups in so short a time that made them so readily available; whatever it was, it was unremarkable in Liverpool to go to any notable venue and see a nationally recognised act. Geno Washington and the Ram Jam Band, Eden Kane and Freddie and the Dreamers were successive acts booked by the Silver Blades Ice Rink where I spent many a Saturday night. It was interesting doing the Stomp in skates!

Nems record stores, owned by the late Brian Epstein, were another good place to hang out. The first was in Great Charlotte Street and the innovative thing about it was that you could ask to listen to a track from a record before buying it, in one of four or five booths ranged along the side wall. You could, in fact, stand there all day listening, without having to buy anything. Since records were less affordable in those days (a 'trannie' and Radio Caroline being the nearest thing to free music) it was a novelty that had Nems packed to the doors on a Saturday afternoon.

Clothes and make-up were as inspired as the music. The new fashion for tights hitched hemlines higher and higher, and two pairs of knickers were required, one over and one under the tights to give a tanned bare leg effect from a distance, and to ensure that the crotch of the tights didn't sag like long johns below the mini hemline. Imagine the indignation of the nuns when one of our Fourth Year pupils, Toni Skellen, was on the front page of the *Daily Mirror*, with a Quant-cum-Sassoon bat-cut: the dark hair was swept forward in a Beatle style with three deep points cut into the fringe like bat wings. She was my heroine for days, or at least until I discovered that she came from the suburbs and her father owned a night-club in Bold Street. It was then I think that I realised it's not what you know in this world but who your dad knows.

I spent most of my time trying to replicate those Twiggy eyes. White powdered eyeshadow was first applied all over the eyelid. Next one of up to three pairs of false eyelashes was applied with eyelash glue – that also came in handy for securing tendrils, or 'corkscrews' of hair around the hairline, a face framing style, with a bun at the back for those of us who didn't have the Toni Skellen mop and were trying not to be jealous. Black eyeliner was indispensable, for this was where the real artistry came in. First the false lash line had to be elongated into a Cleopatra-like sweep at each side; then ever so carefully, under the false lower lashes thin black lines were drawn in their shadow. The effect was spidery and stark. Finally, the eyebrows having been plucked away almost entirely, a thin eyebrow was drawn in a brief but deep arch, reminiscent of Jean Harlow in her prime. A very black waterproof mascara would finish the look, blending false lashes with real.

The success of companies like Biba, who started making clothes very cheaply in that short shift style made famous by Jean Shrimpton, gave those of us who could thread a needle or crochet the inspiration to produce our own; and even if things did not quite turn out the way they should have, they could still be passed off as a trial fashion of sorts – so much was being welcomed as new that mistakes were probably the origins of many trendy modes. It was a good idea if crocheting a dress to get the more intricate and dense flower patterns over the boobs, particularly if one was going bra-less. The problem with this particular fashion as far as I could see was that there must have been many girls, myself included, for whom going bra-less went unnoticed. To raise the desired eyebrows, a minimum of a thirty-six inch chest with nipples like ice-cream cornets was a prerequisite.

As neither of us had substantial bosoms, my sister and I turned our creative talents to interior decor, which was also going through a revolution at the time. We attacked the magnolia gloss of our bedroom door and wrote PSYCHE-DELIC SHACK in big wobbly letters (to give the effect of an LSD hallucination) and coloured them in poster paint – lime green, purple and orange. My sister tore up the lino and carpet, scrubbed the floor boards and gave them five coats of yellow gloss paint. The walls were emulsioned orange and green and we dutifully hung our posters of Che Guevara, David Bailey and Warren Beatty. For our dressing screen (a cardboard affair for hiding dirty washing) we spent hours cutting out multifarious pictures and phrases from magazines: martini bottles and phrases like 'This Is Where It's At' were typical. In retrospect, I wonder how either of us, snuggling under our matching red and black striped Mexican blankets, ever got a wink of sleep in that throbbing colour scheme.

It seemed like it was summer for such a long time in 1967, the year of 'Sgt Pepper's Lonely Hearts' Club Band'. Essential uniform had become Levi's (*not* Wranglers), black polo necks and black PVC jackets, pale panstick and even paler lipstick. We must have looked like droves of the undead moving round that highly fashionable triangle of Liverpool pubs: The Phil (Philharmonic), The Cracke (Ye Olde Cracke) and O'Connors. At that time the penultimate in drinking sophistication was a glass of Black Velvet – the ultimate was a pint. Ex-member of the Scaffold Roger McGough and Adrian Henri could often be found holding court in O'Connors, producing what were to become highly regarded poetic works – poetry that summed up the youthful rebellion against war, racial prejudice and sexual repression. It was the time when Liverpool was the place to be and we knew it.

And did all that upheaval in living standards, in attitudes and fashion have a lasting effect on the lives of the adults who were teenagers in Liverpool in the sixties? I believe it did. It gave us tolerance for new ideas, and brought us a step nearer to equality of rights, removing many prejudices of sexual, racial and moral origin. It gave us the freedom to accept or reject things on their own merits and according to our own individual preferences. I believe that the sixties were a mini-renaissance in which the right of individual expression was encouraged, applauded and nurtured by a generation whose naïve belief was that all we needed was love.

Terri Quaye

Taking It on the Road

And so the sixties arrived finding me continuing to live in the room I had rented at the other end of the street to where my family lived. Although I had finally escaped from the anger and violence of my celebrated father, I was still overrun by my innate feeling of responsibility and protection for the family I had left behind. The best I could come up with was to provide a sanctuary nearby.

Having a father who was a celebrity in the world of showbiz was no easy task – it meant always living a double life – having a subconscious ethical code not to dispel his stage image of the carefree, happy-go-lucky entertainer. Being the eldest child and surrogate mother to my brother and sister, I was privy to the struggles of the family. I understood that this code was not only to satisfy my father's pride but it was also necessary in order for him to work – family violence by one of London's top jazz singers would not prove to be much of a box office draw.

Being from one of the very early Black families in Britain had its own code too. There were so few of us, that instinctively we became one extended family. Having been bombed out of the East End and evacuated to North London in 1940, we found ourselves as one of the first Black families in Finchley. This nascent community consisted of three families who instinctively became an extended family – staying intact, supporting, comforting, protecting and enjoying each other. All the children addressed the family adults as 'auntie and uncle' and their respective children as 'cousins'. As a courtesy any white friend introduced by an 'auntie' or 'uncle' was afforded the same honorary title – a signal that although this was someone from outside the 'family' they could be trusted and confided in.

Here I must introduce you to the most important and influential person of my life – my grandmother. Gran was white and from the East End. She above anyone else gave me my feminist perception from as early as I can remember. For her no challenge was too great – she feared no one. She could neither read nor write, yet she took on racism and prejudice wherever it dared raise its head within her vicinity. Throughout my schooling (as the only Black in the school), she would constantly rebuild my pride in being Black and in being a girl, after each racist attack. She had defied her community twice, by having a Barbadian husband, and after his death a Jamaican. Gran had also acquired a reputation for keeping a 'safe house' for Caribbean seamen on leave. Having her as a constant companion gave me a steady diet of integrity, pride and humour and the obvious respect and gratitude she received from our extended Black family provided me with an everyday example of successful integration against all odds.

For her, if you didn't understand that a woman was the superior of the species, then quite frankly you had something missing! Her perception was crystal clear and immediate, with unhesitating generosity. The war brought our family the bitter-sweet ordeal of being bombed out of the East End. For Gran there was no romanticising of her fellow working-class Eastender. Her memories included being mobbed and humiliated, while stones were thrown through windows for marrying a West Indian. So our evacuation was our ticket out of Mosley's breeding ground.

This had been the beginning of Black Britain. Ties with 'back home' were kept alive by the yearly exchange organised by my grandfather at Christmas. From the end of the war, we would send a parcel of clothing to his family in the Caribbean and we would get in return the most exciting parcel you could imagine. A knock on the door and the postman announcing 'Is this parcel for you? I'm afraid the string's broken, and there seems to be something sticky coming out of the bottom' signalled the beginning of Christmas. It was all my gran could do to stop me going berserk with excitement! Then came the long wait until my grandfather arrived from work. 'It's here! It's here!' I just couldn't believe how long adults took to open a parcel. Our isolation became a precious privacy as the parcel finally unfolded and on to our table came MANGOES, PAWPAW, BREADFRUIT, A COCONUT, SUGAR CANE and black, black Christmas cake dripping with rum. We were home.

By the beginning of 1960, however, change was well on the way. Britain's Black population was now established and springing up in various parts of London, but the feeling of an extended family gave way to that of a separated family – a family in trouble.

News filtered into our communities about the Blacks in America and their insistence on claiming their identity. I remember how proud I felt and how instinctively they seemed to rekindle that sense of extended family, so that I too felt part of that struggle. The sense of isolation was always present – I was born here, but not from here. I was visible yet invisible.

I was beginning to tire of the struggle I had with my hair. In 1960 hairdressers still visibly weakened and verged on hysteria if you walked in with Afro hair. Straightening had been the solution since I had been eleven years old. This had been my mother's way of trying to give me some independence from the work my hair needed to look right. I remember how I had sat in front of the hairdresser's mirror and watched as she combed a burning solution through my hair – stroke after stroke, stroke after stroke, for two hours. The tears would well up inside me as the pain became too much to bear. I would then cough and swallow and say 'can you stop for a little while'. She may have noticed my knuckled hands gripping the arms of the chair, but being polite she'd say 'I'll just lift the hair so that some air can get to your scalp and cool it down'. And after a rest and a cup of tea we would start again. I would remind myself that when it was over I could at least now use the combs that were on sale in English shops, and comb my hair without pulling at the roots or struggling with the many knotted curls until my arms ached and I dropped exhausted into a nearby chair in tears. I could now buy women's hair lotions that would feed my hair and scalp and try to repair the dryness of skin that Black people have in this climate. There were no hair picks, no large-tooth combs, and the selection of dressings available in British shops to cope with this 'invisible hair' amounted to Brylcreem, English Lavender Brilliantine or old faithful Vaseline. And so I sat and endured this transformation every six months, paying two guineas to accommodate the simple desire of being able to groom myself.

I had been born into a jazz musician's family. Life was built around music and the music business. From my very earliest years I had been encouraged to follow the family line of musicians. That encouragement came to an abrupt and violent end however when my father got frightened and saw me as competition. So here I was in 1960 – moonlighting!

After nearly losing the sight of an eye from my father's graphic attempt to stop me being a musician, I had taken an office job. My exit from home had meant leaving a small brother and sister to cope with this chauvinistic tyranny and a mother unable to condone any form of parental questioning. Nothing less than blind loyalty was expected – in my case quite literally. But as always, there was Gran – the invincible – who administered the delicate removal of my belongings from the danger zone by systematically wheeling them out of the house in a covered shopper under the enemy's nose. There was parental relief that I had at last come to my senses and the coast was clear and unchallenged again. The status quo had been firmly re-established and my father could once again relax upon his musical throne in safety.

However, what was really happening was that I had taken a job in a book publishing office to learn to understand office skills and contracts. I needed to prepare for that career I intended to have. My childhood had been dominated by theatrical agents claiming their dues, bailiffs walking off with the furniture and my father trying to figure out the fine print he had missed in the contract. So here I was – gathering survival skills in the day and singing in secret at night.

When I say in secret, this was because both he and I were making the same rounds in London's Soho. I picked the jazz clubs where he no longer sang and where I could be fairly sure he wouldn't turn up. Ronnie Scott's Club was taboo. I would have to take a chance and keep my eye on the door if I sang at the Downbeat Club in Old Compton Street, but the safest was the Mandrake off Wardour Street. Here I was invited to sing with a good house band and build up my repertoire ready for going on the road. In those days any familiarity with Soho meant getting acquainted with 'the girls'. They plied their trade up and down Old Compton

Street, Wardour Street, Gerrard Street, Frith and Dean Streets. The Mandrake Club was smack bang in the middle of the 'business' section. It was here that I had my first real taste of female solidarity. I had made friends with many of the prostitutes who would come in off the streets to get warm, have a drink and listen to the music. I got to know their favourites and in return they made me feel special. I remember one evening struggling to be heard over the voices of a rowdy crowd of men. I remember feeling such despair at the lack of musical appreciation. Then in walked Beryl and Hazel. Both took up their bar seats and waited for the noise to quiet down, but it didn't. Finally Beryl – Black and six feet tall – took the microphone and announced 'this girl's trying to sing. One more word and there'll be trouble!' She handed me back the microphone and signalled to Hazel, then they both took up positions on either side of the club while I finished the set to a silent audience. Hazel died soon after of TB, but if Beryl should ever read this, the thank-you still holds twenty-eight years after. I began to get a steady following and the Mandrake started to do good business – but as with all good jazz stories the singer pays the price and, unknown to those who applauded, I was getting the princely sum of 'a bowl of spaghetti each night' – sing for your supper!

But times were changing – the music business was booming, jazz and rich melodic harmonies were the food of the day. Devotion to finding the chord or note which would convey exactly how you felt and fill the air with emotion was paramount and if this was how you presented your music the reward was total respect and understanding from both audience and fellow musicians. Dance bands were still in full swing, with London's Astoria and Empire Ballroom packing them in every Saturday night. This was where the jazz musicians would don their tuxedos and best behaviour to play restrained versions of the melodies that they would improvise on during the week at pubs which were running small jazz clubs and bursting at the seams.

Women musicians were rarely seen except in the Ivy Benson Orchestra – an all-women band. We had cornered the singer's market but then came the brick wall. However, not to be deterred, I introduced my drums into the arena. I had been playing for years, but now was the time to come out! By now my father had joined his family in Ghana, so all I had to contend with was the anxiety and panic of male musicians in general! Drummers needed the most counselling. If they were able to calm down at all after playing with the only woman conga drummer around, this was generally towards the end of a gig. They usually found that, in spite of themselves, they had enjoyed playing, got off their behind, stopped posing and invariably played better than usual. A smile of relief said yes, they would take a chance on playing with this woman who sang and played drums again (but don't come up with any fancy solos).

This territorial hysteria had, however, the unmistakable signs of being a predominantly British disease. Having been brought up enjoying a cosmopolitan exposure to international musicians – most of whom were American – the contrast was and still is, profound.

British musicians were thirsting to know 'how to relax and let the music flow'. My favourite pastime was to hang out in the basement of Dobell's record shop to hear the latest American imports – Ernestine Anderson's 'Toast of the Nations', Chachito's 'Ace High' and my favourite, Ahmad Jamal's 'Poinciana'. It was this sense of musical maturity that helped influence Britain's popular musical taste. Another contribution to the unstiffening of the English ear was the accelerating Caribbean influx and with them – Blue Beat!

Blue Beat was the music of the young Blacks of the sixties. It was the predecessor of reggae and was competing with the then familiar calypso which would repeatedly rear its mischievous head at Lords during the cricket season. With Blue Beat came the rent parties where the rare adventurous English tasted Caribbean hospitality and let their hair down as they danced – rum and coke in one hand and a plate of curried goat in the other. The room was usually cleared for dancing except for a few chairs around the walls and illuminated by a coloured bulb. Mister and Mistress Whoever held fort in the kitchen where there seemed to be an inexhaustible supply of food and drinks. Once the party was in full swing, they might be persuaded to leave their posts for a turn round the floor, to their favourite calypso, accompanied by shouts and applause from contented guests. The extended family began to gel again – this time with the aid of Melodisc Records, the Blue Beat label and the first imports of Jamaican Red Stripe Beer!

By 1962 I was regularly appearing in London jazz clubs but still working through the day. I was now working at Esquire Records – a small independent label run by a dear friend, Carlo Krahmer, a jazz drummer of the forties. Carlo was blind and I would spend hours reading music gossip from the then jazz musicians' mouthpiece *Melody Maker*. At Esquire I picked up more in-depth information about surviving with a music career, particularly copyright and small record deals which I continually filed for future reference.

Although being Black in Britain meant that you constantly had to be on guard for unsolicited attacks or abuse, we had a continuous supply of inspiration from our Black American cousins. 1962 was like a rescue mission. The Harlem Globe-trotters took England by storm – I thought I would have lost my voice cheering – and still more was to come in the most wonderful sight and sound of the Duke Ellington Orchestra. By the end of 1962 I'm sure I'd grown four inches taller!

The following year came Broadway's all-Black gospel show *Black Nativity*, followed by Ella, then Ray Charles. At Esquire Records I had been joined by Paul Jones who was also picking up recording expertise. In the evenings Paul would rehearse with the group Manfred Mann and a lunatic singer called Mick Jagger, while I doubled between the jazz groups at the Mandrake Club and the Contessa Club on Archer Street. The Contessa provided the perfect opportunity for me to sing and play congas with the latin-jazz group of Ido Martin. There was always a constant supply of musicians who wanted to sit-in, just to play this beautiful combination of music – our guests included George Shearing, Amando Peraza, the Errol Garner trio and countless others who would rush there when they finished just to catch our last set.

Meanwhile, the pop scene had now gone into full swing. The BBC were fighting off the inevitable and sticking their fingers in their ears to the birth pangs of groups like the Beatles. Elvis Presley had been bad enough but surely this, being undoubtedly British, could be a threat to the Empire!

I was now with the Gunnell Agency, who managed many of the day's pop stars. My job was to help publicise and promote Georgie Fame and the Blue Flames. His music was a mixture of pop, soul and jazz, drawing heavily on such people as Mose Allison, Professor Longhair of Louisiana and Louis Jordan. This was the kind of pop music that I could relate to, with its roots firmly planted in jazz, and in fact I often played with Georgie's group at the Flamingo.

This was now the swinging sixties – apparently all hell was breaking loose, but it made little difference to the Black community. The release from society's constraints only applied to the young whites, and as with most phenomena, those enjoying it would find it hard to believe that it was of little consequence to those only permitted to be onlookers. The swinging sixties for the majority of London's Black community meant Rachmanism. When doors slammed shut in your face and accommodation agencies code-marked your name as 'undesirable', a room could always be found by Rachman – with all the perks which ghetto housing brings – humiliation, despair and anger. Racism was again accelerating because there were now too many of us to be invisible.

My father never returned to our family and so I moved back home to help support them. Gran was now an experienced telephone user and, being able to write numbers, had appointed herself as my secretary and booking agent. It was 1963 – time to pack up and go on the road.

Alexandra Pringle

Chelsea Girl

I was a young girl in a famous part of London, but for me it was simply home. The territory of my childhood lies between the houseboat stretch of Chelsea Embankment and the Notting Hill Gate end of the Portobello Road. The westernmost point of this world was at Chelsea Football Club, which was and is our club; and in the east our land ended at Harrods – a sort of barrier, and not really our shop, though we went there occasionally.

Shops always seemed my special neighbours, and two shopping streets stand in my memory now. The first is the

King's Road. A hundred yards behind it is the house where I was born, a Georgian cottage with four rooms, a basement, and the attic which was mine. There was an outside lavatory in our garden until the council came and built a bathroom. The second is Kensington High Street, a sort of grand conduit for the values of school, the route of my daily journey on the 49 bus for my dreary days of confinement to education. I have never liked Kensington, because Chelsea in the 1950s was so happy for a family. In the King's Road, with its tall plane trees, squares of white-fronted houses and red-coated pensioners, we Pringles did our Saturday morning rounds together. I remember Jones the grocer, where there were glass-topped biscuit tins, Timothy Whites, Sidney Smiths the drapers, and the Woolworths with its counters piled high with sweets, where my brothers and I would buy construction kits of Panzer tanks, or pencils, or hideous shimmering calendars with uplifting subjects for birthday and Christmas presents. There were also quite sedate expeditions, for me, when my mother and I went to the Kardomah Coffee House following missions to Peter Jones for dress patterns or fabric. Naturally, it was here I was later taken, a thin embarrassed thirteen-year-old, to buy my first, unneeded, brassiere.

My brothers were my best friends. In the street-corner shops we exchanged huge old pennies for gob-stoppers, liquorice sticks and sherbet fountains. The Essoldo Cinema had double bills which were often not for children. In St Luke's playground, once a churchyard, we hopscotched over the old graves and perfected our techniques with the yo-yo.

There could be no such pleasure in Kensington High Street. It was a place of self-control and respectability, with no hint of the raffishness and cosiness of Chelsea. Here I walked in a crocodile of little girls in grey pudding-basin hats, all holding swimming costumes rolled up in towels. It was a street where everyone wore school uniforms – even, in my imagination, the grown-ups, with their recognisable patterns from Barkers and Derry and Toms.

I remember a day which – I suppose – must have been cold. I

was on the swings in St Luke's playground. A friend's mother asked me if I felt different, changed in some way. Today, she said, is the start of a new decade. I thought she meant a new century, and this was how I learnt of the beginning of the 1960s.

Gradually the King's Road began to change. A new clothes shop opened. It was called Bazaar and my mother would stop sometimes to talk to its owner, whom she'd known at art school. Her name was Mary Quant and her hair was cut in a curious geometric shape. My father reminisced about the days when her husband, Alexander, played the trumpet in the Express Dairy. I loved to hear of those old bohemian times, after my father had been demobbed from the King's African Rifles, and my mother had left the ATS – in which service she had learnt the skills necessary to fast driving in lorries. I knew that they were a generation of young men and women who had caught up with life in the years after they had been in the war. There were tales of wild exploits, like Tambimuttu chartering a plane to Paris, where my father carved my mother's initials into a tree; and I could not tire of the stories of my mother and her best friend Marcia, two beautiful art students giggling in their life class, sewing each other into 'thirties evening dresses with rigid bosoms, stepping out to mock their suitors. Such lovely reminiscences they were, of artists and plastered poets in the French Pub, of my parents' new-wed romantic poverty.

The early days of the sixties were romantic, to me, in a different way (drinking in Soho bars was to come later). Suddenly the King's Road was full with new and unlikely people, all of the magical age in which they were adult but not old. From Bazaar, remarkable at first for the simplicity of its lines, came the mini-skirt. This smallest of shops reached fame through the very *smallness* of its garments. Local residents stared and pointed as young women catwalked up and down the King's Road. It was these women of Chelsea who fascinated me then, not the men. They wore big floppy hats, skinny ribbed sweaters, key-hole dresses, wide hipster belts and, I believed, paper knickers. They had white lipsticked lips and thick black eyeliner, hair cut at alarming angles, op-art earrings and ankle-length white boots. They wore citron coloured trouser suits and skirts that seemed daily shorter. They rode on miniature motorbikes. They had confidence and, it seemed, no parents.

I wanted to be like these brilliant creatures, but was far too young: besides, I was a schoolgirl and had enforced early bedtimes. My brothers and I saved our money for the Beatles' first single, the very first, and we saved and saved for a whole LP, 'Hard Day's Night'. Mark couldn't make up his mind between Millie and Cilla Black. My difficult choice was between Paul and John. Formerly (I say modestly) among the very best of all hula-hoopers, it was easy to do the twist. The shake and the hitch-hiker were not beyond me either. But the glamour of the sixties remained elusive: my skirts were too long, my legs, my mother said, too thin. I was 'square'. Emboldened by photographs of the new model Twiggy, one evening, secretly, I shortened all my skirts. My mother admitted defeat with some laughter, and things looked up.

In 1964 my father stood for Parliament for the second time. What a joke, how hopeless, the Labour candidate for Tory Westminster. I stood on street corners, glowing and brave with pride, to hand out leaflets. Vote for Daddy! Vote Pringle! Such a handsome man, said the ladies in the Tachbrook Street committee rooms, as we folded thousands of red election addresses (with a photograph of the candidate's family) into their envelopes. One evening, surrounded by press, my parents went to canvass the servants' quarters of Buckingham Palace. No one had dared before. In our cavalcade of a blue Triumph Spitfire and red double decker bus we drove through the quiet streets of Belgravia, where there are no shops, laughing in the faces of the rich (who shook their canes at us), up and down the Embankment, then home through friendlier Pimlico. We knew the enemy: those parents at my brothers' speech days, with their Kensington chins and conventional hats. At school little Mark defended the Pringle honour in a fight with one of Maudling's sons. Labour will win, anything can happen, even the puny can win.

And then, Kensington began to lose its stuffiness. A small shop had opened on the Abingdon Road which was to end its days in that bastion of old-ladyhood – Derry and Toms. Perhaps it was the greatest frivolity of the sixties, but to me it also seemed awesome. It was black and gold, it had brothel-like interiors of palms, ostrich feathers and glittering sequins. It was Biba's.

At the very beginning Biba was a hang-out for dolly birds of the Cathy McGowan variety: long fringes and large spikey eyes under hats studded with holes like Emmental cheese, in shifts made from upholstery fabrics. But as it moved from a backstreet to the main thoroughfares of Kensington, a certain lasciviousness, a sort of voluptuousness crept in. Crowded into dimly lit communal dressing rooms, now proud of the leanness that made every garment fit me better than those around me, I tried on clothes for the sinful and *louche*: slithery gowns in glowing satins, hats with black veils, shoes stacked for sirens. There were shoulder pads huge as American footballers', evening dresses to make Betty Grable sigh, make-up – chocolate and black – for vamps and vampires. And for real life there were raincoats to sweep the London pavements, tee-shirts the colour of old maids' hats, dusky suede boots with long zippers. I cannot remember my first Biba garment, but imagine it was one of those autumn-dyed tee-shirts. I do remember a navy maxi-coat I wore to Paris (the men shouted *Napoléon* after me), a trouser suit stolen from a harlequin, a black crêpe blouse with billowing sleeves, a halter top growling with leopard spots.

Kensington was now the place of fashion – more chic than Chelsea was. For the King's Road was awash with flower power. Saturday morning shopping expeditions and lunches at the Chelsea Kitchen were accompanied by the tinkling and tinkling of cow bells. Psychedelia vibrated from Sloane Square to the World's End where a shop sign informed us 'Granny Takes a Trip'. Men with long curling hair showed off their Mr Freedom velvets. Brightly buttoned into military jackets (my brother John caught impetigo from his), tall in platform boots, necks hung with Indian scarves and beads, the men were now the peacocks, the strutting confident creatures of the King's Road. Or perhaps I simply had more of an eye for them.

Almost before we knew it the village of my childhood had disappeared. One could not even buy the ordinary stuff of life in the King's Road. There was no grocer any more, no fishmonger or butcher. Dozens of new clothes boutiques stretched down the street. Shops came and went so fast you never remembered their names. Even Bazaar disappeared. There was no glamour now, only tat. The old residents of Chelsea were squeezed out, including us. We went to live in a gloomy mansion flat off the Fulham Road. I took the bus to suburban Putney and school, where academic failure was confidently predicted. I sank into a curious adolescent apathy that lasted until I left home, and London, in 1971. I was eighteen, and the Tories were in again.

AN INTERVIEW WITH
Joan Fletcher

Morning in Wales
....

I was born in 1949, so I'm thirty-eight now; my sister is four
years younger than me, and my brother six years, so I was the
eldest. My dad is Welsh, he was one of twelve children; some
of them went down the pit and some didn't. My dad was a coal
miner. My mother was a farmer's daughter; she did various

small jobs, but it was mostly housework until we were grown up, teenagers.

I went to Llangollen Secondary Modern until I was fifteen, then I totally refused to go to college. I'd had enough of education. Jobs weren't hard to come by. First when I left school I went to live in Rhyl in North Wales and worked for six months in a hotel in the bar with women. Then I came home and stayed for a while, I went into tailoring – I made Chester Barrie suits for Harrods. Then I did a bit of machining, making frilly underwear, but I worked in a club as well at night, a working man's club, behind the bar. Then after about three years I came to London, working for hotels in the West End. Then I met John.

Things were a lot easier in the sixties. I left school and I was earning £3.11s.11d. I gave my mum £2 and I lived on the rest. And oh, we had some really good times. I was never frightened. It's funny now, because I wouldn't let my daughter do these things. We used to hitch up to Manchester and go to this club – the Twisted Willow Club. We'd just get lifts. I used to go to a club in Chester, and it's still there. It was on three floors and we used to go every Monday night. Monday was my night off. It was the best night. We used to get all the American groups there, like the Drifters. Benny King I saw there, Fleetwood Mac and so on. It was just a stage, a small stage you could step on to. They used to come out and have a drink with you in the bar. It was not like in London where they're sort of separated from the crowd. This was everyone at the bar together. It was great. And there was jazz upstairs; Kenny Ball and his Jazzmen used to come there often.

Every Monday the same little old man used to pick us up. I used to go and stand by the bus stop. The chap used to come in his Morris Minor. You'd get in the car and he'd say 'Hello.' That's the last word we ever got out of him until we got to Chester and he said 'Goodbye.' Coming back there was a man who used to have a Capri. For twelve months the two of them – one would take us and one would bring us back. I never knew their names. The coming back one, in the end he'd come and pick us up from the door of the club and take us all to our own houses.

I've always been pretty independent. I used to just – look I left school when I was fifteen, I was fifteen in the April, I was working in the August. As soon as that happened I was regarded as an adult. There was nothing in between. Once you left school you were an adult and you were working. That was it. It was very strict up until I left school; but then suddenly I'd left school and I'd go home on a Friday or Saturday and say, 'I'll see you Sunday.' 'Oh, right. Where you going?' 'A gang of us are going to Manchester or Liverpool.' On bank holidays fifty or so of us used to hitch to the coast in Wales and sleep on the beach. Or whatever. 'Well, as long as you're in company.' That was it. The trouble I could have got into. You know, we were innocent. I think sometimes a lot of it was being a bit naïve. We used to do things without thinking. I mean even those big pop concerts, the open air pop concerts.

I was very into clothes too. Mini-skirts. I always remember making bermuda shorts – orange with big black spots. I went out the house and my dad was standing on the step shouting 'Your knickers are showing!' It was these bermuda shorts, bright orange. All up the road, 'Your knickers are showing. Where's the rest of that skirt?' I remember big earrings, thick high heels. And eyeliner, that peel-off eyeliner. Oh, it was weird stuff. It used to sort of come in a bottle like nail varnish and you painted it on and it went like cellophane. And then you'd go flipping about and the whole thing would come off in your hand and you used to end up with one eye. And Mary Quant, everything in black and white. Levis were the thing. If you had a pair of Levis – oh. And Hush Puppies. Levis and Hush Puppies. I cut all my hair to half an inch once. It came up like a crew cut. We used to have all sorts. My daughter's far more conservative than I ever was. I did some modelling too, just local, just for a laugh. I was like a stick of rock. I mean, I had no shape at all. Like Twiggy, but it never looked quite right to me.

Then I used to go to clubs, and people were smoking dope. I've smoked pot and tried a couple of things. Nobody felt uncomfortable. They had fights, the same as you do, but not like today with knives. And I always remember the youth club. There was always something going on, and everybody was friends and we used to go on walks up the mountain on a Saturday, start off at eight o'clock in the morning. It was nothing to walk twenty miles. I always remember stopping out all night in a barn once. There must have been about thirty of us. We'd been on a mountain trek. We went into this barn and found this old tarpaulin and we slept boys and girls all in a row. What we looked like I don't know but it was a large tarpaulin.

We'd really have a good time just talking, sitting down and talking and listening to a few records. There just wasn't so much materialism then. A lot of the things you miss are places like the old milk bars, where you could just go and sit and have a cup of hot chocolate and put the records on the juke box. Everybody met there. You had friends of both sexes. I mean people used to come from Wrexham to come to our house. My mum used to make egg and chips for everybody. They didn't have to be boyfriends to take them home.

But I think also people were more family-minded. I mean all this and then I also used to go to this club and do ballroom dances with my dad. It's amazing the way old people look at teenagers these days. I don't think older people give the kids as much respect now. They treat them – I don't know – with suspicion.

What I had, I did have a childhood. Even though we weren't well off things in the sixties cost a lot less. Your money went further somehow. Oh, we had good times. I'm not unhappy now. I don't know how I'd be if I'd stayed. I've always been pretty independent. My mum says I was a totally unloving person. I had one thing in mind and that was me, and that was it and I was off. I was very single-minded. I was always one for a bit of wandering about. It's not boasting or – you know, but I was always more cultural. My sister there was quite happy to go to the pub three times a week and play darts, but I was never satisfied with just doing that. I had to go out and do other things. Going to concerts. I liked going to the theatre. I liked going out for a meal. You know, they don't bother so much at home. I could never go back and live there, in a narrow community like that.

CHANGING

'These boots were made for walking, and that's just what they'll do'

Barbara Castle

No Kitchen Cabinet

I have never understood the ferment of the sixties I hear so much about. I was barely aware that it was going on. One of the reasons, I suppose, is that I was too busy. Action is the great antidote to frustration, which the ferment was supposed to be expressing, and I was not frustrated. I was fulfilled. Having been a political animal all my life, here I was in 1964: unbelievably a member of the Cabinet and able to put my oar in on all the issues which were stirring people up.

So I was not active in the streets, but in government. While students were demonstrating in the universities against the war in Vietnam I was doing battle against it in Cabinet and threatening to resign if there were a sell-out over Rhodesia.

As Minister in the first-ever Ministry of Overseas Development I took on the Bourbons of the right-wing press who attacked the new Ministry on the grounds that charity begins at home and that economically embattled Britain ought not be giving largesse to 'ignorant natives' who did not know how to use it. Later, as a member of the inner Cabinet as Secretary of State for Employment, I had to face the hard economic choices of government: how to decide which alleviations of inequality must be made immediately, and which must wait a little before they could be met.

Thus absorbed, the shock waves of the sixties going on outside did not penetrate my consciousness. It was not that I was out of sympathy with the new mood. It was just that what other people seemed to find new I took for granted.

I had never for a moment, for instance, doubted that I was as good as any of my male colleagues. An instinctive belief in sex equality was part of the socialism in which I was brought up. I had my self-doubts like everyone else, but they were nothing to do with my being a woman. Of course in seeking to fulfil my life's dream of becoming an MP I had had the usual struggles against male prejudice – though never from my father. Its manifestations used to encourage rather than depress me, signs that men were often not as sure of themselves as they might appear. They were huddling together in a freemasonry of mutual sexual support, assuring each other that when a woman stood against a man for any job the man must naturally be the better bet. By the time I was looking for a Parliamentary seat the cruder expressions of prejudice had given way to an even more irritating paternalism. It was 1944; the war was nearing its end; a general election could not be far away and constituencies were beginning to look for candidates. I was eagerly looking for my opportunity and I remember a rather stolid, fatherly trade union figure saying to me: 'Of course, Barbara, I believe you would make a good MP, but unfortunately women won't vote for women.' I knew it was a lie and in the event it was women who gave me my opportunity. Blackburn, a winnable seat, was preparing for selection and the women's section of the Labour Party suddenly woke up and announced that it would not do its usual election chores – writing envelopes and making tea – unless there was a woman on the shortlist of candidates. The men bowed to the storm and the women, who had nobody particular in mind, but were acting on principle, then turned to the regional women's organiser and asked her to suggest a name. She suggested me. So I found myself before the selection conference. It was then up to me. I was on my way. I have been in favour of positive discrimination ever since.

Then again I did not feel the need, as so many in the sixties did, to defy convention, shock the Establishment or turn traditional attitudes inside out. My parents had been doing that all their lives and mine. I was reared in irreverence: trained to challenge all the stale assumptions of a class-bound society. How my father held his job as a fairly senior civil servant I will never know: he must have been good at it because he refused to conform, either in his behaviour or in his views, to what was expected of him. No hippie ever looked more unkempt than he did with his badly cut hair straggling down under his battered felt hat, cigarette ash showering on his shabby overcoat, as he sat on the top of the tram on his way to work reading his beloved Greek. Long before I was born my parents had shed all the proprieties in which they had been brought up. My mother shocked the passers-by in well-bred Stratford-on-Avon as she paddled in the river, showing her ankles. The first thing my father did when he married her was to teach her to smoke because it was unladylike.

But it was never just gesture nonconformity. The challenge to conventional ideas went deep. And it was sometimes not easy for us children to accommodate. Children instinctively like to conform: it is more comfortable, but, inspired by our parents, we loyally stood out against the wave of jingoism which swept the country after the First World War, refusing to sing 'Land of Hope and Glory', campaigning for the League of Nations and agreeing with my father that joining the boy scouts and girl guides with their 'fight for king and country' ethics was not for us. We sported our red rosettes at election time, which set us in a world apart at school. We were left entirely free to decide whether we went to church or not, my father making it clear that he was himself a humanist, and spent our Sunday evenings in his study reading aloud together from the *Iliad* and the *Odyssey* and William Morris. We were taught to despise worldly success.

So none of the ferment of the sixties struck any new notes for me. Some of its outward manifestations were amusing enough. I loved the Merseyside sound of the Beatles and went mini-skirted like everyone else, enjoying its impish irreverence, just as after the war I had enjoyed going into the 'new look' with its longer skirts, bouffant sleeves and romantic picture hats which marked our revolt against the functionalism of wartime clothes. I was never into flower power but I was delighted to see young people clamouring for peace. But I could not help wondering why the mood had suddenly erupted and why it was taking some of the forms it did.

One of those forms in particular left me cold. I was out of sympathy with the manifestations of Women's Lib which were beginning to seep over from America and which reached their apotheosis in the seventies. Of course I wanted women to stand up for themselves and to discover their own potentialities, but I became increasingly impatient with their obsession with their sexuality. Consciousness-raising was fine, but was there to be nothing else in their consciousness? The Victorian days of sex repression and ignorance were long since past and most women were no longer in the dark about the facts of life as even I was when I went up to Oxford in 1928. My parents had been too shy to discuss them and in any case my father probably thought we children would deduce them from the wide range of books on his shelves which we were free to read. (I shocked my sixth form mistress at Bradford Girls Grammar School by choosing D.H. Lawrence's *Women in Love* as my prize for being head girl.) But even D.H. Lawrence was short on some of the technicalities one needed to know, so one of the first things I did when I got to St Hugh's, having read an advertisement in the *New Statesman* about a book which would reveal all, was to organise a whip round in the Junior Common Room to buy it. It was in great demand. Since then I had sorted myself out sexually. It had been a bumpy ride but it had brought me to the point at which I could appreciate sex as a powerful, creative and potentially disruptive force, but one which should not be allowed to occupy the whole stage. I had a mind as well as a vagina and I did not see why the latter should dominate – there are too many other interesting things in life.

By the sixties, attitudes to sex had moved a long way from those prevalent in my pre-war years and I did not like the direction in which the women's movement was turning them. I had no use for the sex war and all the nonsense about encouraging women to believe they could only feel big by making men feel small. As a socialist I wanted to make everyone feel big and I believed you could only liberate women by liberating human beings in general. I was irritated by the Women's Lib trivia: the insistence on the use of Ms instead of Mrs and the manufacture of the hideous word 'chairperson'. Men soon learned to mouth *that* one as a concession which cost them little: words are cheap. It is always unwise to go for form instead of content and I don't give a damn if I am called 'chairman' so long as I am in charge. When Labour lost power in 1970 I went on a lecture tour of America and encountered the writings of the feminist predators for the first time. After a spate of their consciousness-raising techniques I rebelled and told the press that if I had spent my time worrying whether I was called Miss, Mrs or Ms I would never have acquired the proud neuter title of Minister.

This was not an élitist view. I knew that few women got into Parliament, let alone became Ministers. And few of them want to. What matters to most women is whether they are given the opportunity to find out what they are, what they want to be and whether they are given the backing by society to lead the lives they want to lead. Real equality must go down to the mundane things, like how do I get enough to live on, do I or do I not have children, who will help me to bring them up? What margin will be left for me to be myself? As Claire Raynor put it the other day, women have the responsibility for begetting children, but who will share the responsibility for rearing them? These are the very stuff of practical politics.

I wanted to be a Minister so that I could influence the response to these questions and it is obviously absurd that there should not be more women in Parliament and government to voice women's needs. But this is not to say that women should be in Parliament merely to represent women's interests. Apart from anything else, those interests vary according to the circumstances in which women find themselves. Mrs Thatcher's would be very different from those of most people. It is hard for anyone, male or female, to fulfil themselves if they are poor, ill-housed, ill-educated and struggling with ill health. Women's special problems must be grafted on to the battle against injustice wherever it may occur.

This is what we were trying to do in government. We had our quota of macho-males, but we had come into office as the standard bearers for the caring society and that was a society from which women would benefit most. And in Harold Wilson we had a Prime Minister who believed in women and positively enjoyed promoting them. So, although there were plenty of reactionary attitudes lurking in Cabinet, it was easy to win feminist arguments. It was symbolic, for instance, that David Steel was able to get his abortion law reform through Parliament and put the 1967 Abortion Act on the statute book because the government gave it time. Incidentally, seven members of the cabinet voted for the Bill on its Third Reading, including Roy Jenkins as Home Secretary, and of course myself; and one voted against. Eleven cautiously abstained.

Another symbolic achievement was when Harold Wilson persuaded me to leave my beloved Ministry of Overseas Development and become Minister of Transport. It was the last job I had ever had in my sights. I am not mechanically minded and I do not even drive, but Harold was shrewd enough to realise that transport was too big an issue to be left to the highway engineers and the motorists and he suspected that a woman might have the vision to put it in its wider social context. In the event, I came to find it the most satisfying of all the ministerial jobs I had to do. To my surprise I did not find the technicalities as intimidating as I feared I would. Civil servants can always handle them. My job was to work out what transport system we needed in this crowded little island in the motor age: how to bring the boon of mobility to everyone. The motor car had been a blessing to millions, but it was also snarling up our cities, damaging the environment and under-mining public transport, increasing the isolation of those without a car, including the housewife left at home while her husband drove to work. It was a problem which taxed my brain, but also roused all my human sympathies. I was not going to have all the department's money swallowed up by motorways. Public transport was still the mainstay of most people's lives. I wanted to make it cheap, convenient and, not least, comfortable: no more standing in the rain for buses which never come, no more struggles for the tired traveller, the old, the disabled, or women with toddlers clinging to their hands as they traipse from railway station to bus stop or from bus station to bus station. I dreamed of bus/rail links and interchanges that would bring Rolls Royce standards of travel to everyone.

Inevitably I aroused the resentment of the macho-motorist, who objected to my invasion of his male preserve. A woman Minister of Transport was bad enough, but one who could not drive was intolerable. Resentment turned to fury when I introduced the breathalyser. I was soon made to realise that the sex war was not dead. Publicans threatened to refuse to serve me if I visited their premises. Darts match devotees sent me abusive letters. 'Three Regulars' wrote to me threatening, 'We'll get you yet, you old cow'. As the Suffragettes found, chivalry flew out of the window when a woman started to exercise power. The saddest commentary on sex relationships came from a woman who wrote to me, 'Thank you for giving my husband back to me. He used to go to the public house alone. Now he takes me with him to drive him home.' Male anger was only silenced when the road accident figures at the end of the first year showed that the sobering effect of the breathalyser had saved 1200 lives.

Throughout all its economic travails the Labour government of 1964 struggled to achieve its new society. A Minister of Technology was appointed and a Department of Economic Affairs set up to plan regional development. Pensions and benefits were increased dramatically, comprehensive education encouraged and university education expanded. A vast housing programme was launched, the redundancy payments scheme introduced. Its fatal mistake was not to challenge the City frontally when it organised a run on the pound immediately on the return of a Labour government. Its answer should have been to devalue rather than deflate and the failure to do so – its decision to try to defend sterling at all costs – led to successive cuts in public expenditure. But this was not a willing choice. Public expenditure cuts were not seen as valuable in themselves, but as an agonising necessity. The building of the new society was not to be abandoned: merely postponed until the economic situation was stronger.

Some of us were deeply unhappy about this policy. I myself was often in conflict with the Treasury and never more so than in 1968 when at Employment I was put in charge of a stern prices and incomes policy. A rigid norm was operating which left no margin for a move towards equal pay. Once again, it looked as though the rights of working women were to go to the bottom of the queue. The situation was saved by the women sewing machinists at Fords who went on strike because they were deeply suspicious about their job evaluation scheme. They were not consciously leading a demand for equal pay, but instinctively the women were revolting against a situation in which the overall differential between men's and women's pay in the firm was 20 per cent. Eventually the dispute was solved by a reduction in the differential, to which the firm was only too happy to agree. Treasury pundits attacked me for the positive role I had played in reaching this settlement. Orthodox newspapers like the *Financial Times* accused me of having betrayed the prices and incomes policy.

But woman had tasted victory. The enormity of the unfairness to women in pay settlements began to take a hold on the public mind. As Minister I had been outraged to discover the pay grading in industries like engineering with its descending order of categories: skilled, unskilled, labourers and women.

I wanted to do something about it and women Members of Parliament gave me my opportunity. The prices and incomes policy was up for renewal in the House and they threatened to vote against the government unless the policy was amended to allow progress towards equal pay. I persuaded my male colleagues that the government would be defeated unless they allowed me to announce its phasing in. And so I was able to put the Equal Pay Act of 1970 on the statute book. It was far from perfect but it was a crucial turning point. My main concern was to get the principle embodied in law before the election which was looming up.

It was the interplay between political and trade union women inside and outside government which had achieved the breakthrough. The tide of opinion had begun to flow in women's favour, but there was a great deal more to do and we knew it could only be done by painstaking legislation to transform the treatment of women in society. In our opposition years, during Edward Heath's unhappy interregnum from 1970 to 1974, we enlisted the help of brilliant social reformers like Brian Abel-Smith, Peter Townsend and Richard Titmuss to plan what must be changed. We agreed that marriage could no longer be regarded as a meal ticket and that women had become independent breadwinners – often the sole breadwinners, shouldering heavy family responsibilities. Legislation must be adapted to take account of this profound social change.

When Labour was returned to office in 1974 we were armed to apply this new concept across the whole spectrum of social policy. Michael Foot, who had joined the Cabinet, started the process in his Employment Protection Act, which not only increased financial help with the costs of maternity, but equally importantly gave women the right to reinstatement in their former job after maternity leave. As Secretary of State for Social Services it fell to me to overhaul the national insurance scheme. The Beveridge scheme was out of date and we had already had one shot at replacing it with a state earnings related pensions scheme. I had to take up where Dick Crossman had left it in 1970 and, thanks to women's new assertiveness, I was able to give women equal rights in social insurance they had never had before.

In order to do this we had to get rid of the concept of dependancy. As long as a married woman could opt out of insurance and rely on her husband's benefits, she was never going to be treated fairly even when she contributed in her own right. So we abolished the married woman's option for future entrants and in return gave women the same benefit as men for the same earnings-related contributions: a triumphant break with the scheme of my Conservative predecessor, Sir Keith Joseph, who argued that women should get a smaller benefit because they lived longer! I told him that if men led as hard-working lives as women, they too might live longer.

I even cheated in the women's favour, giving them the same benefit as men even though they retired five years earlier. I argued that as women would have to live a long time on the pension, it was essential that the pension should be adequate. Ideally men's retirement age should be reduced to sixty, too, but the cost was too prohibitive for us to contemplate at the same time the Act was going through. No doubt one day the European Court will rule that this discrepancy is unacceptable, but in the meantime for a change it is men who are complaining of inequality. The Act also improved the provision for widows and introduced equality of treatment for women in occupational schemes. I even managed to take a small step towards a survivor's pension by introducing a modest widower's benefit.

The second main pillar of our social philosophy was child benefit – a direct challenge to traditional paternal rights. It was founded on the belief that any financial concessions made by the state to help bring up children should no longer go to the husband but to the wife. It started as a straight switch of the man's child tax allowance into a cash benefit payable to the mother. The family as a whole was no worse off but the man experienced a reduction in his take-home pay packet. We intended to build child benefit up gradually into a non-means tested instrument for combating poverty, which bites hardest among the low paid with large families.

Once again some macho male mutterings were to be heard.

Men, we were told, would never put up with this raid on their beer money at a time when they were being urged to show wage restraint. Even when I had successfully piloted the Bill through the House of Commons, Jim Callaghan, who succeeded Harold Wilson as Prime Minister in 1976, tried to get the scheme postponed on the grounds that the trade unions would never stand for it. He underestimated how deep the change in social attitudes had gone, for it was our trade union colleagues who responded to my agonised appeals and saved the scheme.

The new deal for women was buttressed in innumerable ways. The Sex Discrimination Bill was passed and the Equal Opportunities Commission set up. An Invalid Care Allowance was introduced to compensate those – usually women – who stay at home to look after an elderly relative. New importance was attached to social services which set women free from domestic burdens – home helps, meals on wheels, day centres, day nurseries, community hospitals, school meals. There were some serious gaps, of course. It was not possible, for instance, to implement the Finer report on one-parent families, largely because of the cost. But a new pattern of thinking had been stamped on the nation's consciousness.

It seemed at the time that the change of attitude was there to stay and that we would progress steadily towards a freer society. Two decades later the whole process has been reversed: 'Victorian values' are back again, with all their implications for women. 'Self-help' has become the cardinal virtue, by which is meant that public provision of services should be scaled down and women made to reassume the domestic burdens they had escaped. Child benefit is being whittled away in favour of means-tested schemes and school meals are disappearing. Provision for maternity has been reduced, including the right to reinstatement in a job after having a child. Women's low paid full-time jobs are being turned into still lower paid part-time ones. And the bomb is enshrined as the permanent core of our defence policy as a good thing in itself.

The alarming thing is that women are accepting these

reverses almost passively. The protests of the sixites have fizzled out. Revolt has given way to resignation. It is as though women's estimation of themselves has shrivelled under the impact of a dominant woman Prime Minister, determined to turn back the clock.

What has gone wrong? Part of the reason must lie in the unhealthy introspection of the original campaign. Obsessed with self-discovery in sexual terms, most women had little interest in political organisation or in the administrative minutiae of equality. Sexual politics took over from social policy. (It was a mistake that was made by the leadership of the Suffragettes and by Christabel Pankhurst in particular. By conducting a single issue campaign for women's electoral equality she was left philosophically stranded when the vote was won. She had no interest in how the vote was used and never accepted, as Sylvia Pankhurst did, that women's rights can only be secured as part of a shared freedom. She ended her days as a religious fanatic, espousing every reactionary cause.) The revolt of the sixties brushed away many conventional cobwebs, but never struck roots in a comprehensive political philosophy. A vacuum was left for the counter-revolutionaries who had spent the intervening years preparing every detail of an unequal and repressive society. Women are now paying the price for not having armed themselves.

Leila Berg

All We Had Was a Voice

When I was asked to write this chapter, I realised that nearly all the things I remember happened either in the thirties or the sixties. The thirties was a time of anguish, of creeping fear, of crying out, of youth's romanticism, and of bloody reality; the sixties a time of elation. Elation because people were at last speaking aloud their private thoughts and all the separate voices became in a most astonishing way a choir of creative activity. Energy had been unblocked, set free, and it was exuberant. Everything seemed possible.

CND, established just before the beginning of the decade, had heralded the new spirit: CND was joyous then, joyous because people were ungagging themselves, and their boldness was creative and imaginative; and the columns with tugging banners on the way to Aldermaston were happy to find themselves in such stimulatingly diverse company, and were jubilant with song.

(As the years went by, and the politicians took hold, this changed. When I wrote what was assessed by the selection committee as far and away the best Aldermaston song –

I have questions demanding an answer,
I've been deaf, dumb and blind long enough
I have hands that are able and tender
Oh world, give me love, give me love

– the politicians were taking over CND, and 'the best song' was dropped even before it was picked up because it was about other things as well as the bomb: a strange affair. But the creative joy of CND in its first years has never been surpassed; and it signalled a new decade.)

We were living at that time in South London, in a large house on a common. I was running a nursery school there that was benignly supervised by an Old English sheepdog, whom the littlest kid could ride on, and whom one day, out in the garden, they all painted vermilion.

In the front room the CND committee met. The fifteen- and sixteen-year-olds of the YCND held meetings and ceilidhs in one cellar; and we ran magnificent film pro- grammes at weekends in the other, which we had made into a perfectly-equipped cinema, with twenty-three tip-up seats from a cinema that was changing to a Bingo Hall. I remember how deeply disturbed I was when Soviet tanks entered Prague – we had been showing Milos Forman's films. The projection- room was also a guest room for kids on the run, or waiting for an abortion or recovering from one, or coming off heroin.

During this time something happened, a small thing but it impressed me. Our son, when he started grammar school in the fifties, had joined the school Cadet Corps because it offered canoeing; but now he wanted to leave. The Cadet Corps – I had checked at the very start – was a purely voluntary body. I wrote to his head, saying D would be leaving the Corps, as he was now interested in CND. This was the beginning of a long, polite, but acrimonious correspondence, I repeating that I knew the Cadet Corps was an entirely voluntary body, the head repeating that he absolutely insisted boys voluntarily belonged to it. Eventually, since this could go on for ever, I wrote, still courteously, that D would not be attending any more. I said nothing whatever to anyone else. But almost immediately everyone, separately, left the Cadet Corps. In a very short time, this large prestigious Corps, of which the head was extremely proud, was dead, and the head made a very terse speech regretting and accepting this. I was amazed.

The sixties began with the *Lady Chatterley* trial. Penguin published *Lady Chatterley's Lover*, unexpurgated, and were tried at the Old Bailey for publishing an obscenity. Prosecuting counsel in his initial address sent thousands of newspaper readers into incredulous and delighted laughter by earnestly asking the jury 'to consider if it is a book you would wish your wife or your servants to read'. And the stream of 'experts' (the new Obscene Publications Act allowed the defence to call witnesses to speak of the book's importance as literature), particularly since the judge had unexpectedly ruled that other witnesses should remain outside while one witness was giving evidence, continued the theme of individual voices speaking out, and jubilantly uniting. Personally I was thankful that most of the experts managed to say that this wasn't Lawrence's best book. I had other reservations too – the spiteful gratuitous anti-semitism. No one remarked on it; it was respectable. I did later wonder sardonically what would have happened, if the *prosecution* had brought it up. But I rejoiced that Penguin won. They published *Lady Chatterley* at three shillings and sixpence, and we all felt rather drunk.

A year or two later, the same prosecutor, whom the new defence counsel said would make even a honeymoon sound obscene, won his triumph. This was in the trial of Stephen Ward. Many people called it the Profumo Affair (John Profumo was Secretary of State for War at the time), and saw it as a juicy political and sexual society scandal. I read the press reports every day, and to me, as to many others, it was a vicious and hypocritical hounding to death (for he committed

suicide just before the verdict was announced) of an uncon-
ventional, generous-hearted, very talented man, who was
made use of, and then betrayed, by powerful upper-class
'friends'. I wrote a bitter little poem in his memory. This was
very far from elation. People like me were very shaken by the
ruthlessness and evil of his destroyers, and the deadly use
they made of sexual hypocrisy; and it took me a long time to
get over my anger and outrage.

I was then writing freelance for the *Guardian* (as well as for
Colin Ward's little magazine, *Anarchy*). The matters I felt
passionately about sprang into my mind as poems; but people
at that time did not rush to read poems as they came out, nor
hotly debate them; so as each poem came into my mind, I
translated it into prose and sent it to the *Guardian*. They
accepted each, sent me a cheque, and printed it within a
fortnight. In the early sixties, I was nursing my mother-in-
law, who was dying of cancer. Cancer then was still a secret
death, and only the bubbling vitality of the nursery-school
children kept me from despair. I wrote 'Sunday Morning'
about her dying. The *Guardian* took it, sent my cheque, but
didn't print it. Weeks went by and I asked them about it
several times. They said it was 'too strong', 'very strong'; they
were waiting for a day, they said, when all the news in the
paper was good; then readers would be able to bear reading
'Sunday Morning'. After two years, I suggested such a day
would never come. They glumly agreed, and printed it.

I have been wondering now, as I write, why I tie this in with
my view on the sixties. But re-reading 'Sunday Morning' I see
what a deep-felt plea it was – a shout – for doing away with
secrecy and the desire not to know, and the patronising
protectiveness we had been trained into.

It must have been round about the same time that Professor Stanley Milgram of Yale University was conducting his
experiments on how far obedience to an institution could take
you, and on the strain between the violence it could lead you
into and your basic sense of humanity. I read about them in
brief narrow-column reports in *New Society*, in those days
(unlike now) a very dull-looking specialised weekly. I was
galvanised. Here were apparently normal people, who had

volunteered to help research into the link between punishment and learning which was apparently run by an eminent university, actually pressing buttons which would supposedly send a lethal electric shock through someone who wasn't giving the right answer to a question. One volunteer said 'I believe I conducted myself obediently, and carried out instructions as I always do. So I said to my wife, "Well, here we are. And I think I did a good job." She said "Suppose the man was dead?" And I said "So he's dead. I did my job."'

I have written this quotation down from the book of the experiments, *Obedience to Authority*, which came out some years later. It lodged in my mind for over twenty years, but I wanted to be sure I got it down in its terrifying simplicity.

1965 was the year I went to Risinghill School in Islington. I was originally led there by front page headlines in every national newspaper: BAN-THE-CANE HEAD IN CLASH . . . PARENTS FIGHT TO SAVE SCHOOL . . .

Islington, North London, was not a district of delight: two prisons, gutted houses propped up by tree-trunks, 'areas' filled from basement to ground-floor level with rubbish and old iron, dead windows boarded over, the stained newspapers from the market always snarling like quarrelling dogs on your heels – and opposite, Risinghill School.[1] It apparently covered nineteen nationalities.

I walked into the playground. Two fifteen- or sixteen-year-olds, a boy and a girl, detached themselves from a group. 'Can we help you in any way?' 'I have an appointment to see Mr Duane.' 'Oh, we'll take you to him.' And hand in hand they walked beside me, telling me about their school, till we got to Mr Duane's study and found he'd been called away. They said cheerfully and without question that they'd wait with me till he got back. 'Don't you want to get back to your friends?' I said, 'Or perhaps to lessons?' 'Oh no, that's all right. It'd be boring to wait by yourself.' And they continued to talk, very pleasantly, not to each other, but to me.

I'd never met this treatment before in schools. Schoolchildren, particularly in secondary schools, were generally too tied by fear to look after someone spontaneously, too afraid of getting into trouble, of being late for something, of not having 'a good excuse', of breaking some unknown rule.

Mr Duane had been called to a laundry up the road that had been smashed up, the laundry people said, by a Risinghill boy. He came back breathless, sank into a chair, and immediately some little boys poked their heads into the room. '*Was* it Terry, sir?' they said. 'No,' he reassured them. 'It's all right. It was Terry's brother. He doesn't go to our school.' 'Oh *good*,' said two of them, and a third added fervently, 'I'm glad it wasn't Terry, sir. I'm glad it wasn't our school.' 'So am I,' he said cheerfully, and waved them away. The concern in their voices was not only touching but remarkable.

That evening I went to a parents' meeting, where Mr Duane was giving the latest news. It went at a furious pace, new questions fired before the previous answer was completed. The hall was packed, with national pressmen as well as parents, and someone would suddenly shout to the reporters, 'Just speak the truth! You can stay if you speak the truth!', and there would be a roar of assent. After two-and-a-half hours, when the hall had to be closed, still arguing, still passionately discussing education, the parents streamed into the streets, bumping into one another as they argued or agreed, and clustering into seething knots at street corners. I had been to many parents' meetings, but never to one like that, never to one where uneducated parents were so passionately involved.

Yet the school was closed. Despite petitions from children, petitions from parents, marches to Downing Street, the school was closed. It was closed because comprehensive education was the hot political issue of the time, and the Labour politicians wanted not a good school but 'a good image' ('Eton is only a comprehensive school' was supposed to be a rallying call). And Michael Duane, with his swift announcement that the children would not be beaten, with his accessibility, with his liking for the parents and they for him, was not giving it. Risinghill was definitely not Eton.

Close to the last day, some lads planned to wreck the school. 'If Mr Duane can't have it, no one will,' one said. Mr Duane got them together and suggested they talked to me so that everyone would hear what they felt. So no one did break up the school – only the politicians at all levels. The men who came to move the piano said another school had smashed their piano to smithereens. A teacher said that at a Lambeth school the children tore the school apart on the last day. At another school near Risinghill, the staff had been pelted with tomatoes, and the staff-room set on fire. And at another school, equally near, the children were rehearsing their brass band with their music teacher, and another *teacher* furiously threw a bucket of water over them all. But Risinghill closed quietly, with crowds of children talking in Mr Duane's study, and the toughest kids of all crying in the lavatories.

After two years trudging, with Michael and me in and out of lawyers' offices, and after several people had withdrawn their testimony because they had a job with the education department, and Auden had startlingly refused us permission to use the stanza starting 'All I have is a voice' at the beginning of the book,[2] Penguin published it: *Risinghill: Death of a Comprehensive School*. Again, and even more now, every national newspaper of every political persuasion, television, radio, people in pubs, in fish and chip shops, in hotels, at dinner parties, talked about Risinghill School, about Michael Duane, about comprehensive education, and whether teachers should beat kids.

Salisbury Playhouse asked me to write a dramatic version. I joined them in the Theatre van, and we toured through their educational area, to theatres, arts centres, colleges, universities – and one open Borstal, where they had a theatre which had never yet been used, and a new education officer who wanted to use it.

The play began with dancing and singing in some of the different languages of Risinghill, and the Borstal audience began to get very noisy and itchy-footed. I sat in the audience, very tense, and saw the tension of the cast. But as the play unfolded, the boys fell utterly silent, and the silence continued many seconds after the last word had been spoken, and when they at last began to stir, several were in tears. That was a day that belonged completely to the sixties.

Almost immediately an organisation was formed – S.T.O.P.P., Society of Teachers and others Opposed to Physical Punishment. (It has taken them nearly twenty years of determined campaigning to get corporal punishment banned in England. In 1986, helped by a ruling at the European Court in Strasbourg that the UK was infringing human rights, they succeeded and it has been illegal in state schools since August 1987.) 'Free Schools' (community schools not run by the state) sprang up; one in Islington itself, the White Lion, still survives. The Education Otherwise movement began, taking its name from the Education Act which says that children must be educated in a state school, a direct grant school, a recognised independent school, 'or otherwise', and inspired by John Holt's *Growing without Schooling* in the States. Again the individual voices that joined together, joined over oceans.

Books came from the States that spoke with the voices of Risinghill – Dennison's *The Lives of Our Children*, Herndon's *The Way it Spozed to Be*, Kohl's *36 Children*, Kozol's *Death at an Early Age* (*very* like Risinghill), and many others; it was uncanny and exhilarating. And *Dibs*, Virginia Axline's book, gave us joy. Publishing was exciting in the sixties. It felt itself a part of grass-roots history, inspiring and participating, entering the union of voices, making things *move*.

Bob Mackenzie was fighting the same fight as Michael Duane in Scotland, showing what true comprehensive education was about. His school, Braehead, in a coal town in Fife, was the only one I had ever been to where the pupils' paintings were not stuck on the wall with drawing pins, but beautifully framed and glazed. His school was closed too. Unlike Michael Duane, his supporters won him another school elsewhere; that was closed too.

He and Michael Duane, A.S. Neill and the American John Holt all met for the first time in our house on the common, and talked all day and half the night. All are now dead, except Michael.

Still in '68 I went down to Brighton to cover, freelance, the trial under the same Obscene Publications Act of Bill Butler, poet, and owner of the Unicorn Bookshop, a meeting-place. He too called witnesses – poets, novelists, professors – to the importance of the books, many of which were in any case on sale or loan at bookshops and libraries throughout the country. But the prosecuting counsel directed: 'the magistrates will know a dirty book when they see one', and he was found guilty. The chairman of the magistrates said he was utterly appalled that people had come down from the university – from the faculty – to defend this filth, and he hoped his remarks would be conveyed to the university authorities.

Outside the court were numerous little bookshops crammed with *Pin-Up, Tabu, Bizarre Sex Underground*, and the local Odeon was showing *Lust in the Swamps* ('oozing with depravity'). Brighton's film censorship board (for some reason the Fire Brigade Committee) had banned *Ulysses*.

Among those who did *not* withdraw their testimony in the Risinghill affair was someone who became an educational editor at Macmillan. He asked me if I would do a series of first books for primary school children. It was common knowledge at the time that the majority of English children did not grow up into adults who read books for pleasure. It seemed to me that the fact that the first books the majority of our children saw were so paralysingly dull, and that this same majority was not allowed to be *in* books, was relevant.

I wrote some sample stories about a London family in a district that was a mixture of Islington, Brixton and the East End, and took them along to an East End primary school. The effect on the class of seven-year-olds I read them to was extraordinary. They laughed like a very small child laughs – helplessly. They laughed till the tears streamed down their faces. They stood up and jumped up and down hugging themselves . . . and hugging their neighbours. I waited for the laughter to subside before I read on; it never did. I read through it, one story after another, marvelling all the time at the very young looseness and floppiness the children's bodies had taken on, and the quite extraordinary quality of their constant laughter. I had often read stories to children, and they had often laughed, but not like this.

I was bewildered, and was still puzzling over it when I got home. Waiting for me was a letter from a head in Kettering to whom I had sent a typescript of another story I'd written, and his report of the scene in his classroom was identical. He said one boy, whose father was 'just the amiable layabout Dad of your story', was trying to explain to the boy next to him, whose father was a 'stern conscientious worker-type', why the story was so funny and so important to him, but he was laughing so much he could only jump up and down, tears streaming down his cheeks, and gasp out, 'It's my Dad! It's my Dad!'

Standing with his letter in my hand and considering all this, my mind went back to the evening I had seen the play *Billy Liar*. Billy lives with his mother, father, and Gran, in Cherry Row in a Yorkshire town and, having recently left the art class at the local Tech, works for an undertaker. He copes by hurling himself into wild fantasies whose energy – or, as often, inertia – ends in real mind-boggling disasters of a domestic kind. Keith Waterhouse wrote it as a novel in 1959, in the funny-desperate-angry style that has now become second nature to us but was new then, and afterwards, with Willis Hall collaborating, turned it into a play which ran for a year and a half in London's West End.

The laughter in the theatre was continuous, drowning all dialogue, and completely physical; I came out not only angry and frustrated since I love the play, but bruised all over from the helpless backslapping and knee-thumping I'd been subjected to from delirious stangers. (It was at this time that Albert Finney, playing Billy, who understood the phenomenon as little as I did then, walked to the footlights and told them furiously that if they didn't shut up he was going home.) Now I put the three experiences together, and it suddenly clicked. The physical laughter of release from tension, the laughter of acceptance, of recognition. For the first time, with a shock of joy, those children, and those adults, had seen themselves portrayed in preserves that hitherto were middle-class and alien. They didn't have to pretend to be someone else any more. They were released.[3]

The first reaction from teachers to my books was horror.

'To carry the idea to its logical conclusion no doubt some of the books must contain phrases like "Drink up your meths, Dad", and "Sis, Sis smoke your pot" . . .' 'The head of the family should not be made the object of criticism. Even in families where the father might be lazy, it does not help to have the point driven home . . .' (It had never occured to me that that's what this funny story was about.)

A head wrote: 'The moral content is degrading. Ask yourself: Did your father stay in bed, and allow the roof to leak? Do you hang washing on the stairs and light the house with unshaded lamps? Do not underestimate the penetration and susceptibility of the young intelligence. Try again, and endeavour to set a standard that the youngster can emulate to his profit.'

One head sent her copy back, with a ring round every 'And' at the start of a sentence. I pointed out that a book I suspected she used with approval began almost *every* sentence with 'And' – the Book of Genesis.

The heads and teachers said that the things I mentioned in the stories did not exist. They said children did not play on bomb-sites or dumps; there were no bomb-sites or dumps; they had all been built over long ago. All children played in parks or pleasant play areas. No children played in old cars. All homes had hot and cold water and proper bathrooms. And nobody used tin baths. Most horrifyingly, they said the children agreed with them. These remarks were made by heads and teachers who actually taught in areas where the children *always* played in the local dump and in the old cars, and had homes without hot water, and used tin baths. (They made them hostilely. Such remarks were also made by progressive university educationalists who quite amiably asked, 'But does any child play on a bomb-site or a rubbish dump now? Have children of today ever seen tin baths?')

It was easy to laugh at many of the letters – almost impossible not to – until you remembered that each letter represented an attitude towards the identity of several hundred captive children and their families, that was obliterating and contemptuous.

One head, one of several I had a television discussion with, picked up a *Nippers* book by the corner (*Nippers* was the name of the series) and holding it up fastidiously between finger and thumb, little finger outspread, said to me confidentially, 'But tell me, Mrs Berg, *would you allow your own children to see it?*' It echoed the *Chatterley* trial.

I heard from the head of a South London school that the six-year-olds often had the job of taking the toddlers and babies to the doctor. So I wrote a very small story about a five-year-old going to the doctor by himself (I'd realised by then that the complete truth would be too extreme). A head wrote denouncing, not the situation, but 'repeated errors connected with the subjunctive: *I wish my Mum was here*. "Was" should be replaced by "were". This is followed by the appalling use of the accusative with the verb "to be" – "*Now it's me!*"' They didn't seem to *hear* anything.

As I wrote later, in my book *Reading and Loving*,

> If you exclude from a child everything that makes reading meaningful – his own speech, his parents' speech, his friends' speech, comics, genuine letters, his spontaneous comments on things that have happened, football pools, matches, Gran dying, visits to hospital – all the things he genuinely enjoys and the things he genuinely hates or is frightened of, if you state you are appalled at his colloquialisms, if you call the content of his life 'disgusting rubbish', why should he confide speech to paper – and ever read or write?

Almost immediately, by chance, came official reports, followed by television documentaries and articles in the national press, showing that the dump round the corner *did* exist, that children *were* bathed in tin baths, that nine out of ten houses in a Nottingham area had no bathroom and eight out of ten no indoor lavatory. And for a moment I sardonically thought we might – miraculously – be respectable.

Still many teachers said if it was true it shouldn't be mentioned. But very many other teachers acclaimed the books with delight and said they had been waiting for them for years ('We laughed till we cried, the children and I'). Voices speaking up, again.

This was another burst of creative, exciting publishing. Against all traditional publishing patterns, I put artists and writers in touch with each other; they actually met (to the outrage of the conventional Art Department). So much communication was hitherto unheard off – and maybe has been disallowed again ever since.

The decade ended as it began, with a trial, the *Oz* trial. *Oz* was a young people's non-authoritarian paper, like *Ink*, *Rolling Stone* and *IT* (International Times). It was not a children's paper.

There had already been a women's liberation issue of *Oz*, edited by Germaine Greer. The magazine editors had then suggested a *School Kids'* issue, and invited any 14–18 year olds still at school to contribute all the contents, without censorship. The result was an issue which included a lot of words that would not be used when the headmaster was present, and pictures that might be drawn on the board but would normally be rubbed out before the teacher came into the room, and a general feeling that school pupils were angry at being patronised, humiliated, muzzled and beaten.

The three adult editors, Richard Neville, Felix Dennis, and Jim Anderson, were thereupon charged with conspiracy to corrupt public morals, and with possessing, publishing and spreading obscenity; the case came up at the Old Bailey, with a fourteen-year-old described by the prosecution as 'the Conspirator', or 'the Accomplice'.

I was one of the nineteen witnesses called by the defence. It was summertime, and I had put on a lilac dress with white collar and cuffs thinking it looked wholesome and demure, with a touch of the nurse about it. This startled and outraged the prosecution (similar outrage arose during the Risinghill affair when I dressed somewhat like the head teachers I was among). It apparently made them feel I was a spy and an imposter, standing there 'in a mauve dress', saying I did not think *Oz* was corrupting, but I certainly thought this trial was, that it was only elderly men who were obsessed with dildos, and that when I was a schoolgirl I read and sold a magazine called *Out of Bounds*, a very angry magazine got out by public schoolboys. One of its most frequent demands was 'The Right to Masturbate'. This puzzled and amused me at the time since I had never found any obstacles to masturbating, and it was some time before I realised life was different for public schoolboys. Its editors were the nephews of Sir Winston Churchill.

The *Oz* trial was far more bizarre than the *Lady Chatterley* trial of ten years back – but anyone who laughed or smiled in court was instantly pounced on and removed (unless it was at one of the judge's witticisms) and it was infinitely more vicious. It was the longest obscenity trial in history (six weeks against *Lady Chatterley*'s one), and at the end the three editors were sentenced to imprisonment.

Even while it was going on, the *Little Red School Book* was prosecuted, and the publisher, Richard Handyside, found guilty of possessing obscene material. The L.R.S.B. originally appeared in Danish, then in Finnish, German, Norwegian, Dutch, Swiss, Swedish, American and English editions, with Italian and Spanish editions in the pipeline. Its tone was quite different from *School Kids' Oz*, very gentle, reasonable, infor-mative and disarming (it is still, twenty years later, a delightful little book), and it is difficult to say which must have angered the establishment more.

Remembering my anger at the *Oz* trial, and at the Stephen Ward trial, and remembering that during the Risinghill affair I said to my editor that there were times when anger was the only worthwhile emotion and that obedience was the English vice, I am surprised I first thought that the emotion of the sixties was elation. Well, it was both.

As the decade ended, I was writing *Look at Kids*, a book interspersed with many photographs. One of them is of a little girl peeing in the street, standing near three small boys.

When I was a child in the twenties, living in a street where boys peed against walls, or high-spiritedly or arrogantly *over* them, I was angry and jealous that I couldn't do the same. It was effortlessly beautiful, that rainbow curve, and I was prevented, arbitrarily, from making it. I used to practise secretly, trying to get hold of the skin to make it go *up*; but it wouldn't. Many years later, in the sixties, I talked about this with my twenty-year-old daughter and her friend and found they had each done the same. This is the only kind of penis envy I have ever met, and it is probably widespread. The text this street photograph fitted into sprang from this memory.

The photograph, taken in a street in the sixties, shows the little girl, obviously trying hard, not peeing *up*, but sending out an astonishing strong jet forward. I don't know how she did it. She was an indomitable pioneer.

I started *Look at Kids* with a description of a baby I saw in a doctor's waiting-room: '. . . the passionately working mouth that opened wide for a shout! But the shout was soundless. Nothing. What was it the baby meant to say?' And I ended it with 'Only children, and the sheer brilliance of children, can save each one of us from the sickness and the death that we choose to call living.' The photograph on that last page was of a hunched old man, isolated, bitter perhaps, shuffling past a long scabrous city wall. On the wall was chalked, in childish writing, 'I like you'.

That – as well as the music and the travel, the world-wide club, the LSD that intensified experience, and the feeling at last, which school had ruthlessly denied them, that they were valid and loving (which is what it was to my son's generation), and the reverberations of Martin Luther King, and Paris, and Vietnam – was what the sixties were about. But it was hard sometimes.

Notes
1. Throughout this section, I've renewed my memory from my book *Risinghill: Death of a Comprehensive School*.
2. This was a shock, taken with everything else. Apparently Auden did not want to see the poem around any more. It had been published only the year before in Penguin's *Poetry of the Thirties*. We decided we could legally use just one line without needing permission. But Larry Kramer quoted *two* stanzas in *The Normal Heart*, in 1985.
3. Some of this section, and what follows, is remembered with the help of my books, *Look at Kids* and *Reading and Loving*.

Frances Molloy

On Our Way to Derry

An extract from *No Mate for the Magpie*

A didn't work for the parish priest after that on account of the fact that he give me the sack. The nixt day a was back in Belfast lookin' for a job. Me search, as usual, led me inte wan cul-de-sac after another, so be the en' of a year in which a tried out twenty or more dead-en' jobs, a was fast becomin' the most spectacularly unsuccessful person in the whole of Belfast (that is, if ye don't count the wile shockin' big important high-up man be the name of the Reverent Ian Paisley that a nearly had the pleasure of meetin' on the day a done me protestant day's work).

Paisley was bein' more unsuccessful than me on account of the fact that he was tryin' te stap some students outa Queens University from goin' aroun' way placards demandin' that catholics be given basic civil rights. Ivery time he tried te stap them he only made things worse for himsel' because the newspapers started te come along, an' the TV way their cameras, te take pictures of the students peacefully marchin', an' the wile shockin' big important high-up man shoutin' things at them about the scarlet harlot of Rome, which was wan of the nicer names he had for the pope.

In no time atall the newspaper headlines were fulla nothin' but the protestin' students, an' iverybody in Northern Ireland was talkin' about them, an' dependin' on whichever foot they happened te dig way (catholics believe that protestants dig way the wrong foot), sayin' that the students were the divil himsel' or god's only answer te all the problems in the land.

For a wheen of months te begin way the only people that went out marchin' were the students themsel's and' a wheen of the lecturers outa Queens University, but as people listened more te the things that they were sayin', ordinary people started te join in too, for the students were callin' for the en' of discrimination, sayin' that iverybody should have a right te a house an' a vote an' a dasent job regardless of what their religion happened te be. They said that Stormont was a protestant parliament for a protestant people, an' that for fifty years, catholics had been treated as second-class citizens.

Well, when this news broke, a lot of ordinary people were surprised te learn that they had been citizens all their lives, an' not only citizens, but second-class citizens too at that. My god, they were sayin' te wan another, te think that all this time we have been only wan step down from the tap an' didn't know it.

They were delighted so they took te the streets in their droves, an' a went way them.

The first march a went te was in Derry on the fifth of October nineteen-sixty-eight. That march turned out not te be a real march atall on account of the fact that as soon as we tried te move aff from the Waterside station, all two thousand of us, we foun' our way blocked be a cordon of polismen lookin' wile fierce. We tried te go by another route, but the polis were there too. The people who organised the march toul us that they didn't want a confrontation way the polis so they just hel' a meetin' instead.

After the meetin' was over wan of the speakers toul us all te go home quietly, but that was aisier said than done because the polis had us herded in on all sides like sheep in a pen on a fair day. Wan of the big head polismen had earlier warned all the weemen an' wains te lave the crowd – because they were plannin' te murder only men that day, a suppose.

Some of the people in the crowd that had come for the march weren't too happy way the polismen for roundin' us up and makin' us stan' in the wan place without movin', so they said te the polismen, S.S.R.U.C. The polismen weren't too happy way the crown for bein' there atall so they started te chastise the crowd be beatin' it over the head way big batons.

The crowd begin te bleed an' scream an' tried te run away, but no matter which direction it run away in, it was met be more polismen way batons. As soon as the crowd began te break through the big throngs of vicious polismen way batons, it was met be a very strange monster indeed, the like of which had niver been seen on the face of Ireland before. This big hideous monster that charged about at seventy miles an hour like a terrible dragon on wheels breathin' out ferocious spurts of ice-coul water way enough force te knock the heaviest man imaginable clean aff hes feet was called Water Cannon, an' the people allowed that it was no mistake atall that it had the same initials as the minister of home affairs because they both bore a strikin' resemblance te wan another.

Later on that night in a pub in Derry, a new song was wrote

76

an' be the en' of the week half the second-class citizens in the
north of Ireland could be heard singin' –

To Derry we went on October the fifth,
To march for our rights,
But o what a mess.
They beat us with batons,
They beat us with fists,
And they hosed us all over with water.

Because a hadn't seen me ma for a long time, an' because it
was a long journey back te Belfast, an' because the weather
wasn't very hot, an' because a was feelin' terribly tired, an'
because a was drooked te the skin, an' because a was droppin'
down dead way the hunger, a decided te call in on me family
after the march on the way back from Derry.

Me ma couldn't have been more pleased te see me if she
hada tried, because just before a landed in the door she had
been watchin' the news on television an' she had seen me bein'
grabbed be a big hefty polisman way a cudgel in hes han' an' a
look of murder on hes face, so she thought a was a goner.
After she was finished huggin' and' kissin' me an' examinin'
me te make sure that no bits of me were broke or missin', a
had te explain te hir how it was that a had managed te escape
from the big hefty polisman way the cudgel in hes han' an' the
look of murder on hes face be tellin' hir that the big hefty
polisman way the cudgel in hes han' an' the look of murder
on hes face had niver had a hoult of me atall but only the back
of me coat that had got me inte all the trouble before in
Belfast way dear an' Alex an' mother, an' how it was that a
had managed te run away from him, an' the coat, glad te be
rid of the both of them, an' how a hoped he enjoyed ownin'
that coat more than a did.

A didn't have a job te go back te at the time so a decided
that seein' as me ma's reception was so cordial a might as well
stay on at home for a while. Very soon a become a fulltime
listener an' looker at the news on the wireless an' television,
an' an expert switcher from wan channel te another wheniver

somethin' interestin' was announced, in the hope of hearin' it all over again on the other side.

Nearly ivery night, the television studios would be packed full of all the wile big important high-up people of the day, sittin, discussin' the latest developments, an' this wee student girl outa Cookstown be the name of Bernadette Devlin, would be sittin' up there beside them all, talkin' rings roun' the lot of them.

A stayed at home all over Christmas an' the nixt march a went te was in the new year. It was a long march that started in Belfast on the first of January an' took four days te get te Derry. A joined it when it got te our town on the third day. At the bottom of our town the polis tried te stap us from gettin' through but there was such a crowd of people in the march that by just standin' tight thegether an' pushin' we managed te break through the cordon. In no time atall we were all headin' up the road in the direction of the nixt town, singin' –

We shall overcome,
We shall overcome,
We shall overcome some day.

Deep in my heart
I do believe
We shall overcome some day.

Ivery now an' again we passed by housin' estates an' the people come out to look at us. At some estates they would be shoutin' encouragement an' givin' us cups of tay an' mince pies an' pieces of Christmas cake, but at others they would be hurlin' abuse at us an' callin' us effin popish scum. When we walked along chantin', wan man, wan vote, they jeered back at us, wan man, wan woman, because wan of our members was reputed te have a slightly unorthodox sex life. We just waved an' shouted, Seasons Greetin's an' Happy New Year back te them, but they spit at us as we went by.

That night the marchers stapped te rest in a town about ten miles outside Derry. A went home te spen' the night an' rejoined them in the mornin'. There was some great excitement in the crowd that day because ivery body was lookin'

78

forward te arrivin' in Derry in the evenin'. When we set aff, bright an' early, we were singin' –

We're on our way to Derry,
We shall not be moved.
We're on our way to Derry,
We shall not be moved

Just like a tree that's
Standin' by the water's side
We shall not be moved.

Some time between ten an' eleven a-clock that mornin' as we were all marchin' along, singin' an' chantin' in quare form allthegether, a big head polisman way a loud hailer an' a blackthorn stick, stapped us along the road an' toul us that there was a small group of Paisleyites waitin' ahead at Burntollet Bridge an' he expected them te throw some stones as us. He said that the best thing for us te do was te link arms way each other an' keep movin' forward way our heads down an' not te panic because hes men had the situation under control an' they would do iverythin' in their power te protect us. We all linked arms an' moved forward like he toul us, singin' away as we did before –

We're on our way to Derry,
We shall not be moved.

Wheniver we landed up at the bridge, it soon become clear te us all that the big head polisman had got hes facts wile terrible wrong. The small group of Paisleyites that he toul us about turned out te be a wheen of hundred strong. Some of them were wearin' the helmets an' uniforms of the 'B' specials an' they were all doin' a war dance an' chantin' as they charged down the slope at us clutchin' crow bars, an' clubs, an' coshes, an' cudgels way big rusty six-inch nails stickin' outa them, an' gaffes, an' bill hooks, an' scythes, an' picks, an' pitchforks, an' partisans, an' many other kine of wile dangerous lookin' implements too numerous te mention.

Up in the field above the road it wasn't just the Paisleyites that had gathered te greet us, because ivery wheen of feet, these big heaps of heavy rock, that had come from a quarry down the road, were sittin' stacked up waitin' for us too. The marchers weren't prepared for anythin' like this size of an attack so a lot of panic broke out when they seen what they were faced way.

Some of them run away back in the direction we had come from, some of them jumped over the ditch on the left han' side that sloped away down te the river, an' some mad mortals like mesel' who really did believe that we could not be moved, stood our groun' on the road for a while an' kept on singin' our song —

> We're on our way to Derry,
> We shall not be moved.

As soon as the rocks started te bounce aff us, we collectively come te the hasty conclusion that maybe Derry wasn't the place we were headin' for atall, so some of us started te rise te the occasion by up-datin' the words we were singin' —

> We're on our way to heaven.
> We shall not be moved.
> We're on our way to heaven,
> We shall not be moved.
> Just like a tree that's
> Standin' by the water's side,
> We shall not be moved.

Wheniver the Paisleyites heard this song they made it known te us that Derry wasn't the only place where they intended we shouldn't go.

A have always been of the opinion that a body has te die sometime, so when a was hit on the back for the fifth time way a rock that winded me, a fell te the groun' an' lay there way me arms wrapped tight roun' me head, thinkin' that me number was up. A suppose a should of been sayin' me prayers te save me soul from iverlastin' hell, but the only thing a could do at that time was think of me poor ma an' all the trouble she musta went te havin' me, an' hope wile hard that she would be able te get over me tragic death, an' that the memory of it wouldn't blight the whole rest of hir life on hir.

As a was lyin' there thinkin', somebody that called me a fuckin' Fenian bastard started te kick me an' rain blows down on tap of me way some heavy implement that a could feel but didn't risk lookin' up at, despite me curiosity. Then somebody musta come te save me from me attacker, for a heard another voice, just as the blows stapped, sayin' are ye tryin' te murder hir, ye cowardly bastard ye, can't ye see that she's only a wain? Me attacker set te the man that was tryin' te save me, an' the man that was tryin' te save me said te me in a wile urgent kine of a voice, if ye can manage te stan', get up now for god's sake, for the coast is fairly clear an' get outa here quick.

A didn't risk anythin' so drastic as gettin' up te run, because a can sometimes be a very cautious sort of a person, so instead a just got onte me han's and knees an' crawled inte the ditch of the right han' side of the road which was the side that the first-class citizens were attackin' from.

Wheniver a got in behine the protection of the hedge, the first thing a done was grope about an' soon a come across another body huddled in there too. It didn't seem te be attackin' anybody so a allowed that it must be wan of us, an' a risked creepin' up wile close te it an' sayin' we mustn't stay in here long, let's get out thegether.

The body then stood up an' lifted me up too way its arm tight roun' me, an' it opened up its coat an' caught my head an' stuck it up inside its jumper. Then it buttoned up its coat again way me inside it. Nixt the body started te edge outa the hedge way its arms still roun' me, an' its back facing up in the direction of the ambush. The body was a fair bit bigger than me but a could still feel the thud of the rocks vibratin' through me wheniver they hit it on the back.

A don't know how long it took us te get across the bridge but it musta been a quare wee while because we were movin' sideways an' couldn't look where we were going'. We kept trippin' over boulders an' ivery wheen of seconds a new batch of first-class citizens would launch a fresh attack te try te finish us aff. Half way across a nearly passed out because a couldn't breathe inside the coat an' jumper, so the body had te loosen its coat at the neck, an' houl down the tap of its jumper te let me get some air.

Wheniver the noise that was goin' on aroun' us sounded at a bit of a distant from the body an' me, we stapped edgin' sideways for a minute an' stood listenin' for a while, an' right enough, we did seem te have come clear of the battle groun'. The body opened up its coat an' a pulled me head outa its jumper an' looked up at its face and' foun' out that the body was a handsome young man way a big bloody gash just above hes right eye. Hes name, appropriately enough, was Armstrong, an' later on that day he introduced me te hes ma, a nice wee worried lookin' woman way a headscarf on hir hair, who had come outa the Bogside te meet the marchers an' look for hir son after she had heard about the ambush on the wireless.

It musta been a miracle, but nobody got killed that day an' soon after we got across the bridge, cars an' ambulances started arrivin' from both directions te help the marchers an' bring the badly injured te hospital

Wheniver this happened, the first-class citizens run away an' nobody has iver been arrested for takin' part in that ambush te this day, even though the polis knew damned well who the culprits were because they could be seen, laughin' and' chattin' te many of them, on the very best of terms, while the ambush was on.

After our wounds had been cleaned up an' the whole area thoroughly searched te make sure that nobody was left lyin' behine dyin', the wans of us that were still able te walk or limp, set aff again thegether on the road te Derry, singin' a different song, an' wavin' blood-stained hankies above our heads on sticks, at the bit that went

Raise the scarlet flag triumphantly

We were movin' much slower than before, an' it stated te rain, just as we were comin' close te' the Irish Green Estate, near Altnagalvin hospital. The first-class citizens that greeted us there were of a slightly different variety te the wans we had just encountered. They were all too feeble te be travellin' te the bridge at Burntollet, because they were mostly semi-housebound housewives way bad legs an' piles an' some terrible big operations.

They reminded me for all the worl' of the weemen outa 'Korea' the day that they attacked the breadman, only they didn't seem as well organised. They had te resort te' pokin' at us way toast forks, an' emptyin' their chamber pots over our heads, so we didn't even bother te bid them the time of day as we passed by.

As soon as we landed in Guildhall Square there was wile commotion. A big crowd of people were waitin' there te welcome us. They shook us by the han's an' asked us wile worried questions about the ambush at Burntollet. Somebody shoved a loud hailer inte me han' an' people started te lift me up on te the back of a lorry te say a few words te the crowd because they thought a was a student on account of the fact that a looked like somebody that had an awful lot te learn.

Wheniver a was on the back of the lorry, me wee brother (the wan that took over me drawer) spotted me an' come te me runnin', glad te see that a was in wan whole piece. After he was finished quizzin' me about me bruises, an' examinin' me te see that no bits of me were broke or missin' (it runs in the family), he asked me was a hungry, an' a said a was, so he took me te a cafe an' ordered a big feed.

We were sittin' there aten when a gipsy woman way a wee ba wrapped up inside a shawl come inte the cafe an' walked up te the people behine the counter. They toul hir that if she didn't make hirsel' scarce, they would get the polis out te hir. She was headin' back out the door again but me wee brother stapped hir an' toul the people in the cafe that she was te be given whativer she wanted te ate an' he was payin'.

After the three of us had finished aten, the wee gipsy woman called down ivery curse an' plague an' affliction that could be thought of (an' a wheen of others as well) on the owner of the cafe an' all the people that worked there. Then she put the blessin's of almighty god an' hes holy mother, an' all the saints of Ireland, on me an' me wee brother, an' we were surely in need of them too, for we were goin' te the pictures.

Now a suppose a body could be forgive for believin', as a did then, that goin' te the pictures isn't a particularly hazardous activity, but that only goes te show how wrong a body can be. As soon as me an' me wee brother said cheerio te the wee gipsy woman, we walked up the Stran' Road from the cafe back inte Guildhall Square an' then turned right through the arch in the wall te head up in the direction of the ABC cinema.

We had only got about fifty yards from the arch when a crowd of polismen way steel helmets on their heads an' riot shields an' batons in their han's, rushed outa an entry an' blocked our way. Me an' me wee brother stapped. Wan of the polismen toul us te get back through the arch. We toul the polismen that we were going te the ABC cinema, an' that the ABC cinema was up in the direction that we were headin'. A polisman called us fuckin' Fenian bastards an' toul us that he would smash our brains out if we didn't turn roun' an' get through the arch. A said te him, that it was a right hearin'-tella allthegether that a body couldn't go te the pictures in Derry without bein' threatened way murder. He lifted us hes baton an' tried te hit me way it but the polisman who was standin' beside him caught hes arm an' said te him, for Christ's sake. A said, thank you te the polisman beside him.

Then a said te all the polismen, will ye's please excuse us, gentlemen, an' let us past, because we want te get te the ABC cinema. The polismen pointed way their batons at the arch an' said, you go that way, dear. A pointed way me finger in the opposite direction an' said te the polismen, now it's clear te me that you nice gentlemen don't know Derry half as well as a do, but please believe me when a tell ye's that the ABC cinema is up that way.

A started te walk in the direction of the ABC cinema an' me wee brother follied me. Two of the polismen grabbed a hoult of me wee brother an' dragged him over te the side, an' said te him, you look like a nice sensible chap, you wouldn't like te see hir gettin' hurt, so why don't ye talk some sense te hir an' get hir te go back through the arch.

Me wee brother said te them, can't ye's just get it in through yer thick skulls that we are goin' te a picture house that is up that way, an' he pointed te it way hes foot. While me wee brother was talkin', a slipped in between two of the polismen that were blockin' me way an' a started te run up the road in the direction of the picture house. A polisman swung hes baton at me head. A got me arm up just in time te save me skull but the blow slowed me down an' the polisman grabbed a hoult of me an' raised hes baton again.

A turned roun' quick te the polisman an' stuck me head in underneath hes chin. A put me arm (the wan he hadn't hit) tight roun' hes neck. The polisman tried (unsuccessfully) te get me te stap clingin' te him. He had a nice new gleamin' weddin' ring on hes finger, so a said te him, a suppose ye'r goin' te tell yer wife when ye get home from work an' she asks ye what kine of a day ye had, that ye murdered a wee girl of five feet tall be hittin' hir over the head way yer baton, just because she wanted te go te the pictures. De ye imagine that she's goin' te be wile proud of ye when she finds out?

He said, look here, a'm not tryin' te murder anybody. Well, a said te him, in that case Mister, ye could of fooled me. A'm only actin' accordin' te instructions, he said. An' a'm only goin' te the pictures, a said. Ye can't go up that way, he said. A can't get te the picture house any other way, a said. A'm only doin' me duty, he said. At the risk of repeatin' mesel', a said, a'm only goin' te the pictures.

A could see that this conversation was gettin' us nowhere so a let go of hes neck an' shot past him an' run as fast as a could up the road in the direction of the ABC but hes legs were longer than mine an' he soon caught up way me an' started te drag me back in the direction of the arch. Me wee brother, who was still bein' held be two other polismen, could do nothin' but shout at me assailant an' challenge him te a duel out in the middle of a big fiel' somewhere where he would soon show him what he thought of men that beat up weemen.

The polisman didn't try te kill me again after that but he still wouldn't change hes mine an' he started shovin' me way all hes might back down towards the arch, but as he shoved me in wan direction, a kept goin' in the other, all the time sayin' te him, please Mister, a want te go te the pictures, a want te see *Darby O'Gill An' The Little People*, a've been savin' up for weeks, gone an' let me go te the pictures, please, please, a beg ye mister, please, let me go te the pictures.

As soon as the polisman shoved me through the arch inte

the arms of the crowd that had gathered te watch from the other side, they all started te hug me an' slap me on me badly bruised back an' tell me how brave a was. The crowd then caught a hoult of the polisman an' started te pull him limb from limb. Wheniver a tried te stap them a nearly got mesel' kilt be me own admirers of a minute before so a went away feelin' sorry for the polisman, because a knew that he was only tryin' te do hes duty be upholdin' the laws that were made for all of us be the acutely deranged, imbecilic, illegitimate, offspring of the mother of parliaments.

They say that bad news travels fast an' a suppose they must be right, because word of my death reached home before a did. When a landed in the back door late that night way me wee brother, a foun' me da sittin' mournin' at the tap of the table way hes head restin' in hes han's, an' me ma rushin' aroun' at breakneck speed, tryin' te make the house all ready for the wake.

Wheniver the two of them got over the shock of seein' the dead alive, they put me inte bed an' a wasn't able te move outa it for a long time because ivery part of me was black an' blue an' bleedin' an' swollen. For the nixt wheen of days all the neighbours kept comin' in te examine me, an' commend me ma for havin' such a brave daughter, because a was wan of only about half a dozen girls that had made it across the Burntollet bridge.

A stayed in me bed for a wheen of weeks an' wheniver a got up a started te prepare mesel' for the future be practisin' some basic skills that a thought might come in useful if iver a went out te look for work again like, combin' me hair, movin' me head from side te side slowly, an' noddin' it up an' down a bit, sittin' down an' risin' up from a chair without bein' helped, puttin' on me own clothes, tyin' me shoes, walkin'. After a was satisfied that a'd acquired sufficient skills, a set out again in search of work, but a decided not te go back te Belfast, as it was clear for all te see that me an' Belfast weren't made for each other so a allowed that a would give Dublin a try instead.

Susan Dowell

A Place in the Sun
....

People ask me whether the successive waves of famine that
afflict the Horn of Africa are 'even more terrible' for those of
us who have lived and worked there. Ethopia was my home

for three-and-a-half years, the birthplace of my own sixties children. It has become as iconised, objectified and remote in its misery as it once was in its obscurity and this has fragmented my memory, turned awe, respect, delight and gratitude for the days of my youth into something that could so easily sound – though never *be* – like Proustian sentimentality. So, I have to believe, that no, it cannot be worse *and* that if we look around us the fragments of the world still seek each other so that the world may still come into being. 'This is no metaphor and it is much more than poetry,' (as Teilhard de Chardin told us in 1959).

I went early in 1964 when I was twenty-one. I had still been at school in 1960 and was taking my own two children to theirs by the end of 1970. The sixties were Africa's Decade, it was said. History had opened up, in the decolonisation process, a precious new space for the young: to go where our white predecessors had gone to rule, to carve out riches and distinguished careers to the glory of the Empire. We could go not to make our lives out there but to share in our hosts'. We did not have to sink our bones or our European identities as selfless missionaries, though we would do useful work, make a 'relevant' (the in-word then) contribution, even perhaps some reparation.

Kennedy's Peace Corps, the expansion of Voluntary Service Overseas projects by the Labour government here, structured this energy. That space is closed off now, specialised and professionalised, discredited, often rightly, as neo-imperialism. Our cheerful amateurist muscle was too close to the economic bone of Western dependence/domination. But I believe that a more generous, imaginative and genuinely good-willed and self-searching response by Western governments could have conserved this space, and that to have done so would have provided a vital resource to the One World consciousness sought today in feminism and other social movements. Instead we have the malice and peevishness which refused long-term development aid to Ethiopia after the 1974 revolution, causing millions of deaths and the near obliteration of entire cultures. The highly individualised communication skills of Greer and Geldof and the practical Aid experts cannot fill the space of the myriad links we imagined, twenty years ago, would draw the world closer together.

> When we are children, growing up in our parents' care, we await the spark from the outside world. Sometimes our parents provide it – if we are lucky – sometimes it comes from another source far from home. We sit, paralyzed, surrounded by our anxiety and dread, hoping we will not have to grow up into the narrow world and ways we see about us. We are hungry for a life that turns us on; we yearn for a knowledge of living . . . We look for signs in every strange event; we search for heroes in every unknown face.
>
> (Alice Walker, *The Civil Rights Movement: What good was it?*)

Strange events, struggle and heroes were pre-packaged for my generation of war-babies. Freedom was something they had already done 'for us'. So an awareness of being a passive oppressor – as white, Western and educated – was hard to articulate, particularly for a culturally deprived (in terms of books at home) girl growing up in the forties and fifties without a robust working-class dissident family tradition. The Second World War really did lay claim to our loyalty in ways I suspect are incomprehensible for those born after it. Films and newspapers poured out memoirs of fearful odds faced and suffering survived. All real. As we got a television set in the mid-fifties stirring documentaries called us back to war-time definitions of heroism, freedom, communal enterprise and national integrity, ossified now by the cold war and the belligerence of a dying Empire. Saturday morning pictures gave us racism too, wrapped up in the adventure stories we longed for our lives to be. 'Natives' were an additional, sinister *frisson* to the thrills of cobras, crocodiles and man-eating lions. This image was confirmed by wireless reports of Mau-Mau insurrection in Kenya. 'That Old White Man' Alice Walker chased out of her head masqueraded, taciturnly

British and self-righteous – no redneck cracker he – as civiliser as well as saviour. Even when writers like John Osborne began to look back at that moral wasteland of the fifties, his Jimmy Porter told us that 'there were no good causes left to fight for'.

My grammar school place – of which my mother was touchingly proud, defying older uncles' warnings about the cost of the posh uniform and 'staying on' after fifteen (so unfair on the boys, my older brothers who hadn't got in) gave me Eng Lit and some sound history, along with the idea that it continued in us: plus a sufficiently nasty dose of fatuity and snobbishness to inculcate rebellion and a gang to be an 'us' with.

I went up, in the autumn of 1960, to Sheffield University, which had a larger than usual contingent of Commonwealth and other overseas students and staff. They turned our eyes from the bomb, which had mesmerised us, or rather helped us see through it and beyond to the imperialism which had created it: created Sharpeville and Ian Smith and the Governor of Alabama. The new heroes whose faces became known – Mandela and his members of the ANC, Lithuli, Kaunda in Zambia and Nyerere, later president of Tanzania – were saying that no, it wasn't too late. Inter-dependence could and would evolve from Independence and change the face of the earth. African political thinkers like the author of *Freedom & After*, Tom Mboya of Kenya, gave us faith in an African socialism which would evolve out of the diversity of regional, home-grown economic structures.

1963 was the year of the UN Freedom from Hunger Campaign. That summer five of us took off, with no money, to beg our bread round England. Calling ourselves Hunger March 63, we reminded people of the time when Hunger Marchers spoke the plight of a Britain divided into two nations. Yesterday (ha!) Britain, today the World. We walked 500 miles, speaking at formal meetings, pre-arranged by our Oxfam sponsors who'd boned us up on some of the statistics, and with anyone who would walk and talk with us. Overseas Aid without privileging pre-conditions, Justice not Charity and above all 2% of the National Income could and must all be demanded of the Labour government waiting in the wings. It was the summer of the great Civil Rights March on Washington and it was good to be walking – blowin' in the wind. So 'what good did it do?' Being there, I suppose, a tangible experience of people's generosity and a willingness to do it again . . . and again.

We said goodbye to the cows and the cuckoos and each other. Krishna went home to India, John to Jamaica and Frances, who'd brought her own nascent feminism to our mission and to me, to study theology at Durham. Of our group two made interracial marriages. Many more of the people I have remained close to from that time did the same. I do want to say here that none of these, Black or white, did so in a contrived colour-blind denial of the very real historical weight their love would carry: although this did alter the issue of whether to marry or just make out together, tipping the balance towards public affirmation and reclaiming orthodoxy as the more creative and committed choice. While none of us would deny that the evolution of Pride, Black or female, and a separatist space, 'for health' as Alice Walker says, is neces-sary and important, there is grief over the dourness and rigidity that has crept in around the issue from both 'sides', back-projecting a shallow tokenism and white-value individ-ualism on to people for whom the eighties are bleak enough. I certainly would not be embarrassing myself here, recording the simplicities of my youth, were it not for the complexities and courage by which so many of my friends have given those hopes a continuing value, not least by their loyalty to one another.

Two of us decided, rather to our mutual surprise after countless break-ups on those foot-sore days, to get married after all. He is an Anglican priest and was offered work in Ethiopia which appealed to him and to me. He is a scholar of Orthodox Christianity and was asked to work with the (fairly) newly autonomous Coptic Church as well as to be Addis Ababa's Episcopal Chaplain to the international community which had recently expanded with the establishment of the Organisation of African Unity and other pan-African UN agencies in Africa Hall: the grand celebration of pan-African development, which had opened in Addis at the beginning of the new decade.

I followed on in time-honoured manner, having completed some post-grad training, going by a French boat from Marseilles to Djibouti in Somalia. All very Channel 4 period location stuff. I'd missed the last flight of the week to Addis and, after some undignified groping and the loss of most of my local currency in the seedy sub-Casablanca hotel I was put up in, this stopped being fun. A war I'd never heard of was going on in this disputed territory as well. No place to reclaim another night and a half, so I made my way to the airport to wait there until Monday. Two Ethiopian pilots getting ready for an early-morning cargo flight befriended me and agreed to let me come along, on my first ever aeroplane. We headed north up the Red Sea to Assab in our tiny DC 2 plane filled with goat skins and me. While these were being exchanged for Red Sea fish I sat under the wing. It was 130°F and the hot air burned in my chest as I gulped it down. I was invited upfront when the fish got on and we flew south, up on to the plateau. We must have skimmed over Lalibela, the eighth wonder of the world, with its 12th-century church hewn out of the rich red rocks, the cruciform roofs at ground level; underneath there is the most perfect, breathtaking balance of space and form I have ever been in. A place of pilgrimage, like many others – but I was off to a wedding. The pilots were amused and delighted to be bride-running and swooped down for me to see villages and *Tukuls*, the round thatched houses, more closely. Here you are: land of Solomon and Sheba.

Ethiopia was always a place to be met and loved on its own terms: offering its own welcome, creating its own distance. Just as it invited Young Africa to grow under its ancient aegis, so too did it cling to its own identity and mystery. So many questions and causes that have preoccupied my life before and since that time were cast in a different light there: sometimes bringing a startling clarity, sometimes a distance and obscurity.

I started off with having the worst ever case of wedding nerves. I was desperately childishly disappointed to find my wedding and my future employment all fixed up and to see so many white people about who seemed inordinately interested in one another. I learned, in light of subsequent experiences in Zambia, that they were a weird, polyglot, brilliant bunch for the most part, dedicated to Ethiopia; and to all those 5 and 10 year development programmes hatched in Africa Hall. It was a very informal and delightful wedding by most standards, but I did not really have any standards. This was the first man I'd gone out with for more than a few months and now I was getting married, among people I did not know, in a strange place. Just like the pictures. Which century was I *in*?

We had a wonderful honeymoon, in a little hut by one of the Rift Valley lakes down south, surrounded by baboons; driving off to Shala and Abyata shimmering in the distance, one covered entirely by pink flamingos. Down to earth for the second week: we dug a reservoir on the abandoned farm which had been given over to the children's home where I was to work.

And that was wonderful. The 'high-powered, dedicated' Englishwoman who'd put in her bid for my services had done so rather reluctantly. She no more wanted a bloody bushy-tailed Christian than I'd wanted to work with Ingrid Bergman and the mutual enlightenment was turned into a friendship which ended only in her death last year.

Our temporary base was a ramshackle house donated by one of the Royal Family. Adanech, who came, medievally, as our 'house girl' along with the house, has steered the whole project through the revolution and the hardships of famine and dislocation. It was set up to provide a half-way home for children needing long-term orthopaedic care, many of them polio and spastic patients. We were taught the necessary – rudimentary – physiotherapy by staff at the local hospital and the Leprosarium. Some of these children were able, after treatment and getting properly fitted with limbs and callipers, to go to their scattered homes, and it is for them my heart sinks when I see and hear of the stricken places. The diversity of the more Nomadic cultures surrounding the central pla-teau was awesome. Resettlement is the emergency name of an age-old, self-defined rhythm: the passivity inevitably evoked in the Western mind is false to the soaring, restless spirit which forever seeks a blade of green. It is impossible not to hope in this: there is land enough if there is the heart, will and true repentance of a post-colonial rich world.

Some of our kids would never be able to leave; they were far too ill and one or two had just been abandoned. I'd never taken pleasure in hard physical work in the way I now could and did. Vacation money-making jobs and Saturday shop work were mechanised drudgery; taking care of a house and children of my own back again in England, even with fulfilling and challenging outside work, often feels fragmented under the gimlet eye of others' (and my own) theories of proper priorities. In Ethiopia the children's fragile health, the ever-precarious state of our supplies and finances, defined each day's priorities and made for a closeness, affection and flexibility between the three of us. I remember best the less-pressured time, in the late afternoon; sitting on the steps in our dusty little back garden, de-bugging heads, giggling as we squashed the fattest, cutting the boys' and braiding the girls' hair into their regional styles. Singing songs and testing out our English and Amharic words on each other. Sometimes shy older sisters and brothers, uncles and aunts, if they lived close enough, would come to visit.

The names children used for their elders, *ti* and *kassa* – my sister/brother, my consolation and shield – seemed to transcend the formal structures of nameable kinship categories. A user-friendly language; though I never learned its grammar and structure in any formal way – 251 letters in the alphabet being rather a challenge. The cultural and spiritual values of Ethiopia had never been undermined by colonialism so there was no moral pressure to 'prove' goodwill and respect by systematic *gnosis*. I was interested in the work my husband was doing with Ethiopian Christians and the development and educational projects in which many of our friends – volunteers like me, and experts – were involved. But I was content to climb out of my head for a while and absorb it all through my skin and senses. (This was a welcome respite from the intense meritocratic pressure I'd been under all my life as a first-generation secondary educated kid: if you have a brain, use it to get on.) We grew close to the peoples' traditions through the seasons and through friendship. The complex rituals of feasting and fasting – fifty-six days of Lent, every Wednesday and Friday no animal products could be eaten by adults – taught us that the knife edge of poverty and the precariousness of agriculture could be honoured and solemnised in community rite. Will the present overwhelming disaster tear away the past as well as the future?

In those days the little and big rains marked out the year and named the children. At the end of the big rains came Maskal, the Feast of the Holy Cross, a time when the ground danced with raggedy-cotton, butter-coloured maskal daisies. At feasts we drank *tedj*, honey-mead, deep-gold, smoky, waxy; ate *injera* and *wat*. *Injera* is made from the local *tef* grain, cooked to form a huge plate on which the hot *wat*/stew is placed. You eat your plate, and your host at the end feeds you a *gursha* – a gift mouthful. We could feed the world this way.

This year I visited Israel and Palestine. There I saw and felt Ethiopia again in the Ethiopian Church on the roof of the Holy Sepulchre in Jerusalem, where the priests keep a lonely vigil among the nations. There are none who understand Calvary, who understand suffering, better today than the Ethiopians. They too are still excluded from the feast and live in small rabbit hutches 'outside the city wall'. Their chapel, small and dimly lit, is enriched by dark, old icons of the Virgin and the Saints, wealth unlimited. Their prayer is constant. Their Christmas feast had to be provided by a Palestinian friend who loves and respects these others who've kept a fierce integrity and distance from the scramble for tourist cash and religious kudos in the Holy City.

Greenham too has restored some of these memories to me: the smell of woodsmoke on my clothes, the all-night vigils, recall the celebration of Ethiopian Easter: tired, candle-lit faces, swaying, singing bodies and slow, slow dancing in a crowded church. A stubborn belief, against all odds and precedents, in the possibility of non-violent revolution was nurtured by Ethiopia. The Italians had committed the most ghastly atrocities during the occupation (when Ethiopian sovereignty was sacrificed to the paper-peace of the late thirties). A whole generation of educated men were butchered. When Liberation came in '41 the Emperor ordered no reprisals and was obeyed. Italians who wanted to stay could do so and did. When the '74 revolution happened it really seemed, for eight months, as if they would pull it off again . . . When I first heard, after more than fourteen years, the ascending spirals of women's keening and ullulating I had a song of my own to add, though I've never been able to properly manage that skylark sound – *lill-li-lilii* – of Ethiopian women as they greet and mourn for each other.

There were dark and terrible things too, of course. The women who trudged the roads single-file, one every mile or so, carrying wood; each burden the length of her bent-double body, twenty-five cents a day, just enough to keep the breath in her body and no man's revolution has lifted her head from the ground. And yes, after a few clumsy attempts to carry the load or give her a ride you retreat. You get used to seeing her.

My two babies were born among women whose bodies were so horribly torn by labours undergone without professional assistance. Many walked fifty miles and more to get to hospital. When the orifices of the lower body become one gaping hole it is called a fistula. This, if repaired, is a skilled costly long-term treatment, perfected by Catherine and Reg Hamlyn, which gives the woman a future in her community. Otherwise in those days she was an outcast, unclean and unwanted. Addis Ababa has a clinic now, built for the Hamlyns to train others, and the aircraft to give a nationwide service. I'm immensely grateful that I owe the celebration of my own body, its strength and fruits to a medical service run by people whose first priority was and is the poor; and, not surprisingly, the experience has made me somewhat sceptical about Earth Mother romanticism.

I was strong and happy to make love, bear children and love other children in a context which did not force false choices or theories on any of us. My beautiful little daughter Clare, named Tsahai/Sunlight, by our closest Ethiopian friends, was two-and-a-half years younger than her namesake in the home: only one year younger than little Alem-Tsahai

(Sunshine of the world) who'd just come to us with both of her hands blown off by an Italian hand-grenade that had lain undiscovered near her village.

Both Tsahais, Adanech and the others left Addis and me when they moved off to the farm and new friends in the agricultural student volunteers who joined the project in this next phase. I had another baby and, necessarily, a more orchestrated life, teaching here and there and developing my new-found passion for drama at the University's Creative Arts Centre. This was run by a brilliant young director, the playwright and poet Tesfaye Gessesse, who gathered a group around him to put on plays and readings. We did Biblical stories, our common cultural inheritance; Wilde's *Salome* – my first lead – auditioned, to my lasting pride and amusement, when I was nine months pregnant, McLeish's *Job*. (Only one line of the former was struck out by the government censor – 'It is a terrible thing, to kill a king. Why, kings have but one neck . . .') Tesfaye himself dramatised traditional Ethiopian epics and sagas. Many of our closest friends then were Peace Corps Volunteers and as we all declaimed the exploits of Theodore and Menelik driving away the invader, they were facing up to the possibility of the draft. It was early days in the Vietnam war then and the tide of revulsion and protest had not gathered momentum. Letters from returnees were full of bitterness and dismay at the direction America was taking under LBJ.

We Brits had our own shame in the Rhodesian crisis. The Wilson government, after a stern challenge at the beginning, hesitated and was lost. When the suggestion came that we go to Zambia it seemed absolutely the right thing to do. Newly independent, Zambia was besieged by white supremacist regimes to the south, west and east. The wounds of the colonial period were open and raw. Still visible were the separate hatches used, less than five years before, by Blacks who had to stand on the street to be served in some of the department stores in Lusaka. There were many refugees from 'down South', Black and white 'rebels' as well as a breed of whites I'd never met before; cynical ill-wishers making a tidy pile out of the fat contracts which the Zambian govern-

97

ment had to offer for Western expertise. For these people the palpable prosperity of South Africa and Rhodesia – propped up of course by Western capital and shameless sanctions-busting – was used to maintain the old, obscene discourse about peoples' 'readiness' for self-government.

After Ethiopia it was really hard to engage in all that. The angry refugees from Zimbabwe and South Africa were, I felt, the only outsiders that Zambians really needed: they knew, for they had lived with it all their lives, the lineaments and history of Zambians' need for affirmation and self-confidence. Zambia had always had the rawest deal of all under colonialism; its population scattered and disrupted by the slave traders and, more recently, all the cultural resources, from the sound effects of its radio station to its museum artefacts and documents, had been centralised in Salisbury – all these names were real then – and not returned when the Federation of Northern and Southern Rhodesia was dissolved.

Some doors did open. My teaching job specified that once the students had reached a sufficient competency in Admin. English they could move on to study literature. Some of the great South African writers, like Ezekiel Mpahlele, were living in Zambia. My classes looked to West Africa too, to the post-independence plays and novels of Chinua Achebe, Onoyo and Wole Soyinka, which gave us a rich field to discover together.

I was especially glad to have gained some confidence in drama. I was drawn away from the indulgences of the mainly white rep theatre to the newly formed University-based drama group UNZADRAM. One of the firebrand émigrée teachers had dramatised Ferdinand Onoyo's *Houseboy* – a powerful novel about the 'servant problem'. We added some Zambian music and songs and took the play on tour. I was the only white actor, though not the only white 'baddie' character – they were all played in chalk-white masks, dead and fearsome. Our first performances were given at the 'national' drama festival in the Copperbelt. 'Welcome to Northern Rhodesia', I was told as our bus entered this bastion of the new Raj. I was asked, quite conversationally, by one of our white hostesses if I'd been sexually assaulted on the bus. Both incidents added something to the performances we gave there. The Black characters thrilled the company with the ad-libs that came spontaneously in the midst of an audience who'd visibly stiffened when required to stand for the National Anthem, words and all. The white characters' sang-froid was called forth when we took the play around the poorer townships, where they spat at us.

We started, during my time, to build a proper Zambian traditional theatre, away from the dreary Westernised town centre. As I left, *Houseboy*'s lead player had just been cast as the Inca Chief in *The Royal Hunt of the Sun* and I heard recently that both strands of Zambian theatre are developing, sometimes together. I remembered them all when we danced with joy at the birth, finally, of Zimbabwe.

What draws us home again? Our own time there was quite consciously short and circumscribed. To be honest I never could feel the passionate, possessive love I have for Ethiopia. We can grow young in old countries and have to grow up in new ones, perhaps. In Zambia the daily, physical fact of living in neat rows in a mainly white street dragged on my spirits, redeemed only by the township community down the road where we worshipped each Sunday. In Ethiopia, we never had to reach out, to make conscious gestures, be 'aware'. Not, I hasten to add, that there is anything wrong with 'gestures', the play was one and I'm proud and glad to have done it. Nor is colonial guilt necessarily futile. What I wanted, needed to do, I realise, was to relate what was, what had to be, the issue of down South to others; the gender and class that I'd been born into and wanted to make mine in ways that couldn't be done as an outsider. Like my students I needed more stories that were my own.

There was one incident which put my unease into focus. A dedicated white Zambian national (taking Zambian citizenship was for locals an important protest against Britain), another clergyman, was photographed outside Westminster Abbey where he was publicising the plight of the hungry and dispossessed in Southern Africa. 'All this must go', he said, sweeping Abbey and all with a contemptuous gesture. For him maybe but not for me. If I had learned one thing, held on to one solid hope, it was this: that the true foundation of the Church, including the Abbey, was Christ and not English Culture: that it could and must be claimed by the poor everywhere. Was this true? 1970 was time to go and find out.

Anne McDermid

Paris in the Springtime
·······································

I became politicised at the age of eight. For many children of my generation growing up in America, the most shocking event in our lives was to turn to our television screens and see, after the cartoons, small children just like ourselves sent bowling down dusty small-town streets, just like our own, by respectable uniformed policemen using fire hoses. The *bouleversement* of our normal perceptions of policemen, teachers, authority figures and the way things work, was colossal. Something had to be wrong. How could these children deserve such treatment by wanting to attend school? It seemed unimaginable that the least offensive members of the society, namely children and their mothers, could be the victims of such appalling brutality, not at the hands of thugs and murderers, but by figures of authority. A teenage boy was dragged by his hair into a waiting police van; a small girl of my own age received a heavy shove which sent her sprawling down a flight of stairs; a woman writhed on the ground while being kicked and punched by burly men; truncheons, heavy boots, helmets, plastic shields, and pistols against flailing arms and legs, sneakers, curly heads. Powerful jets of water from fire hoses took on a snake-like life of their own, and it seemed impossible ever again to chase after those friendly bright-red fire engines as they raced down our street to put out a fire or rescue someone's cat. It was an upheaval of volcanic proportions and made quite a dent in our normal comfortable perception of the rightness of things.

Remember what it had been like before. After the war a stultifying complacency of Christian, white, middle-class and aspiring, suburban family life, two children plus a dog and a cat, squeaky clean housewife/mum, firm but kind breadwinning dad, obedient but cheeky children – this was the world of 'Leave It To Beaver', Doris Day films, the Nancy Drew novels, the nascent advertising industry waxing rich on the production of these endless streams of happy images. This was a world before puberty was invented, where there was no such thing as teenage *angst*, where adolescence was a period of playful banter with parents during which process girls learned how to become like their mothers and boys like their fathers; where pre-marital sex was unacknowledged if rampant, and a young girl becoming pregnant was quite likely to be thrown out of the family home if she did not suffer an illegal abortion. Wives certainly did not work, as they weren't meant to need to. Any organisational or managerial talents she felt the need to exercise could serve to control the constantly proliferating collection of electrical gadgets to prepare food and keep the house clean. Since every man could become President if he simply wanted to enough, poverty only existed if you willed it and therefore didn't need discussing. To question the existence of God was not publicly acceptable and in some circumstances was an arrestable offence. It was certainly an arrestable offence to swear in public, but in fact the local cop spent his time returning lost dogs to their owners and hanging about the local soda-bar, so somnolent was the town. There was no imagining what the alternative was to all that obedience and quiescence except anarchy and chaos. It was a tremendous shock to discover how easily the bargain – loyalty and obedience on the part of the public, to be repaid by protection and the provision of certain basic services, education for example, on the part of the state – could be so easily overturned unilaterally by the more powerful partner.

Much scorn has been poured on the achievements of the rebellious sixties, but surely not by people old enough to remember the terrible stultifying joylessness of the fifties. Of course it is true that in the decade of student activism the only practical freedom gained, among the delusory ones, was the freedom to have sex without marriage. Like the child in the candy-shop, we women over-indulged: with gentle, dope-smoking, mantra-chanting, hippy men; with ascetic, cerebral, intensely poetic men who explained to us all about Nietzsche (we were thrilled); but most of all with the Messianic, charismatic Martin Luther King imitators, the leaders of the Black Movement, of whom we were always slightly afraid, deliciously guilty.

Of course the men thought they had arrived in Libido Heaven. But the hindsights of feminism selectively ignore the great pleasures experienced by women also, for whom it was a time of great self-discovery. It's not useful to think of the sixties as a giant con-trick perpetrated on women, a dead-end we had to get out of; more as part of a process, still evolving, during which women fired their ideas. The same is true of the much-derided little revolt which began in Paris in May 1968.

In the midst of this student activity, sit-ins, demos, and

marches, when we thought we were creating a new way of living, to follow the traditional American students' path and do the Grand European Tour might seem atavistic. Why leave the new society at the moment of its birth to go back to the Olde World? It's a long tradition for Americans to travel to explore their cultural roots in Europe, and Paris has particular associations for Americans in the Hemingway/Fitzgerald/Gertrude Stein community. The café-drinking, intellectual, bohemian life-style symbolised by the open relationship of Sartre and de Beauvoir was the model for the free love society of the flower children. We thought we could reproduce it in Paris, and there being, as usual, a substantial American population in that small city, we very nearly did.

After graduating from the University of Toronto, I had travelled to Los Angeles seeking adventure, and after California French society seemed intimidatingly rigid and formal. There were class divisions we couldn't properly understand and frequently made mistakes about; the standards of achievement in schools for even quite young children seemed very high and the nature of the university education formal and stylised; the level of intellectual debate in bourgeois French households was surprisingly abstract to most of us, as the Doris Day family seldom discussed surrealism and post-structuralism at the dinner table; there was considerably less sexual licence than in the flower power culture and sexual relations were governed by a network of rules making the quadrille look like break-dancing. Parisian women were elegant, coiffed, manicured and coutured, fast-talking and assertive, informed and often witty, and furthermore they were public. Parisian women spent their afternoons at the galleries, then eating *glaces* at the Brasserie Lipp, not ironing the kids' football outfits in the utility room. They seemed very visible. The contrast with the coy and lisping American housewife and the eager but clumsy student was so impressive I didn't notice at first what they were not – Présidente de la République, for example. I had a lot to learn.

There was a large foreign community in Paris, the students of French from other countries, Holland, Scandinavia, Eastern Europe, Turkey and Japan, the au pairs from

England, the cooks and maids from the Basque country and Portugal and then there were the Algerians. Much of my period in France was spent living with a Nigerian I met at a lecture at the Sorbonne. He'd got his degree at Oxford and had come to Paris to pursue his interest in something obscure and philosophical, and his French was better than mine. If I had asked myself why F spent so much time with the Algerians in Paris, when he had so little in common with them, it didn't take me very long to find out. Sorbonne students on the whole spoke to F as if he were a human being, though we were never invited to anyone's home. But walking arm-in-arm with F in any public place was an experience that makes me nervous even now to recall. Intensely hostile stares, venomous hisses, the whispered invective were much more sinister and harder to bear than the American model. At about the same time I read James Baldwin's account of his first weeks of living in Switzerland, when the villagers would come up to him and stroke his arms to see if the black came off, and asked him what kind of food he could eat. In America the battle against racism was bloody, but at least two hundred years of the presence of Blacks forged a worn, contemptuous familiarity. In Europe the fear of this unknown creature, the Black man, was quite naked and new. F and I had both signed on for two external literature courses at the Sorbonne. At the same time I was studying under a distinguished but by then elderly psychoanalyst called Paul Diel. This interest in psychology gave me access to a lot of the content of the later student debates lost on some English observers, but it also prevented my noticing the social dynamic much of the time.,

The French had their own guilt about Vietnam and although very much tinier than the US movement there was a decided student movement against the war. On 1 May 1968 the historic American/Hanoi peace talks were scheduled to begin. Newspapers and coffee table conversations speculated about the potential for these talks, expressed cynicism about the genuineness of American desire for peace, the effect on de Gaulle's prestige for having succeeded in arranging these talks; and I dare say few of us guessed how thoroughly the ending of this most appalling war was to be wiped off the front pages of the newspapers in the next two months.

The first thing about the *événements* is how suddenly they arrived. Not many students at the Sorbonne itself, never mind people outside of the student network, were entirely following the career of Daniel Cohn-Bendit, a German national of French birth at the University of Nanterre, who was active on the left and who was being threatened with expulsion from France. I paid no attention to the initial demonstration in protest against his proposed expulsion, as this kind of thing seemed minor in comparison with the campus lock-outs I had experienced. I was living in a *chambre de bonne* near Trocadero in the 16^e and was, unlike some other students, not very near the university and the centre of much of the activity. However, I couldn't but be aware of the rumours of students demonstrating in the streets and violent clashes with police on Friday night of 5 May. The next morning I went to seek explanations and found that atmosphere of intense excitement, of half-frightened, half-exhilarated enquiry, of strangers talking to each other in the street, of small groups of students standing at corners discussing, of excited rushes from one café to another in the hope of the most updated news, which was to characterise that summer.

Cohn-Bendit's demands for modernisation and changes in the university structure and curricula didn't seem dramatic, but I took them to be a precursor of requirements for an extension of accountability in so many other highly bureaucratised areas of French life. I assumed they were just the start, the first phase of an attack on all the excessively bureaucratised aspects of French institutions; the beginning of a radical demand for accountability and democratisation. But such a thoroughgoing analysis never truly evolved. In fact it seems ironic now how humble were the aspirations, how unambitious the demands which brought down the President when a decade of more generalised disaffection had not. The many historians of the '68 movement – the number of studies devoted to this revolution being bizarrely disproportionate to the number of weeks of history it took up

– discuss at length the process of extension of student demands to a general critique of capitalist society, but this is rather *post facto*. There were many properly argued papers produced, but the expressed demands were always for reforms perfectly consistent with capitalism.

Many senior professors had joined in the demonstration on Friday night but in spite of their presence several hundred people were arrested and were sentenced to jail terms at a hastily convened court on Sunday. The huge *manifestation* in protest at the sentences was my first participation in the events.

It was terrifying. In spite of the wealth of sanitised violence normally available to us through films and television and news accounts of murders in dark places, our exposure to actual violence at an everyday level is very small. Women are more frequently victims of violence than perpetrators of it, but for many of us middle-class students the experience of actual physical activity likely to lead to injury or even death was almost unknown. This probably explains the enthusiasm with which we entered into it. I was completely terrified by how much sheer brute strength is required to drag a parked car from the kerb to form a barrier in the middle of the road; by the shrieking sound of scraping metal; by the force with which torn-down street signs, broken off limbs from trees, anything to hand, was used to lever up the paving-stones of the pavement into small pieces. I cannot now recall the first moment when the weight of a heavy and sharply uneven piece of *pavé* in my hand suddenly assumed the power of a sub-machine gun. But it may have had something to do with the *C.R.S.* I sharply recall the moment when I first came running around a corner and found myself facing a double line up of members of the *Compagnies Républicaines de Sécurité*, the National Security Force originally set up during the Algerian war. I had seen nothing like it, and have seen nothing like it in England to this day. (Although I imagine Mrs Thatcher is working on it.) Armed, dressed entirely in black, heavy helmeted, metal-tipped boots, clear perspex shields, and three-foot rubber truncheons, two impenetrable lines of them, aggressive wide-legged stance. They looked, not just as a group but as individuals, impenetrable, as if they were not human at all but Daleks. Some such thought must have triggered the complete breakdown of customary feminine passivity. I threw my *pavé* with all the force I could muster and the shriek of triumph in my ears was probably my own. The stone dribbled harmlessly to one side, but I had broken a fundamental taboo against civil disobedience which lies very deep. The years of civil rights marching had prepared me for that moment.

Of course I was not alone in that *jetée*, and there were probably as many as fifty of us facing that particular line at that moment. Although there was no sign of movement in the line, shields raised, we fled to our original position behind the barrier of overturned cars. I don't know who first set what alight but only at the first billowing of flames did the line charge, and we heard police sirens in the distance. The possibility of being shot – not hit over the head, dragged by the hair, kicked in the stomach, not suspended from classes or ostracised by relatives – but wounded by an actual bullet fired from a real gun, made those snide comments about middle-class revolutionaries somehow lacking in point.

The Rector called in the police to evict the students from the Sorbonne, an unnecessarily abrupt and ill-considered move, disproportionate to the situation. The students predictably reacted in outrage by occupying the university. The central Amphitheatre became the twenty-four-hour debating chamber for the next five weeks and all the strengths as well as the weaknesses of the movement were played out there. Much contempt has been poured on the ideas generated by this brief movement, the lack of co-ordination between the students and the organised labour movement, their lack of historical basis and *naïveté*; however I think it is easier to make these judgements with hindsight and enormously difficult to attempt to evolve an ideological position in conditions of constant activity – thinking on one's feet. The momentum of street activity had to be maintained in order to hold our position on the front pages of the newspapers and inevitably some decisions were reactive ones. But the atmosphere on the whole was a revelation to me. In French theoretical debate, the concepts of Marxism – and of Freud – form part of the context, whereas in America it would require a monumental struggle to establish the word 'socialism' on the agenda at all. Our debates contained Marxists, Trotskyites, libertarian anarchists, Maoists, but no American-style hippies with their emphasis on life-style instead of theory. It was of course the life-style that the students were really interested in, but their manner and their language was so formal and stylised I was quite misled. It took me a long time to notice how very few women contributed to the debate. They were the same women who, a couple of years later, were beginning to found women's groups and create magazines to address the various issues ignored by the articulate and impassioned young men in the Amphitheatre. I thought the crèche in an upstairs room for the children of the married students (married, you understand; let's not carry the breakdown of society too far) was a truly revolutionary move. F stood up and made a contribution about the treatment of Algerian students which was greeted with polite but slightly shocked silence, only a tiny susurration around the hall. It was as if they knew somehow they ought to be addressing seriously the subject of racism within their own ranks, but couldn't quite bring themselves to face it. On the other hand perhaps they were reacting to F's French spoken with a clipped Oxford accent.

At the same time the Hanoi/Washington talks were proceeding down the road. Apart from a small demonstration outside the embassy when the American Ambassador arrived on 10 May there was almost no acknowledgement of this momentous event. The texts of the May movement had the international solidarity of the world's workers as a central theme, but no demand specific to this war ever surfaced in print or on wall. The Vietnam war, as well as being a monumental world event simply in terms of numbers of lives lost and money involved and weapons deployed, was also a startling example of the enormous imbalance between the power of international capital and the freedom of the individual that students were meant to be demonstrating about. Its symbolic value alone should have been overshadowing and all-powerful. And yet the Parisian students seemed to take on board one side of the equation without the other: they adopted the United States of America as the symbol of Evil and the source of all wrong in the world, without ever mentioning the Vietnamese. But perhaps they weren't ready for close examination of their own parents' role in that poor country.

Somehow the Amphitheatre, and indeed the whole university, came more and more to resemble a prehistoric cave dwelling: hot, increasingly littered with abandoned jackets, papers, bits of food, piles of cigarette ends, an ever-thickening fug of smoke and sweat and yesterday's expletives and faded angers. Filthy, but somehow warm and familiar and comforting. The elegant, disciplined and authoritarian French – many of whom were still going home to their parents overnight – had regressed to an earlier life form: filthy, sensual, anarchic, bohemian – Californian in other words. I felt personally vindicated by this triumph of instinct over intellect.

But I wasn't above brief forays into the outside world for a good meal and a bath myself. I had some aristocratic friends who lived near the Trocadero whose invitations I gladly accepted. It's difficult to imagine an equivalent British family sitting at a table with a foreign scruffy revolutionary discussing the need to involve the workers in the struggle; to formulate demands for improved conditions in the work place and participation in the decision making process and in profits; and to overthrow the father-figure de Gaulle in order to struggle for a new birth. I can't imagine what role these people pictured for themselves in the new regime. I thought of the night of 4 August 1789 in the National Constituent Assembly during which the deputies one by one voted themselves out of existence during the French Revolution.

It was only much later that I realised the difficulties created for French women by their fascination with language and theory, their faith in the power of intellectual ideas. The French women's movement (in contrast to its British counterpart, which was able to articulate some of its ideas around practical strategies and demands) was trapped, because it developed its intellectual machinery within rigid ideologisms, including linguistics; and so it has proved a much longer process for them to come to grips with individual issues.

On 13 May there was a twenty-four-hour general strike. The Renault factory at Boulogne-Billancourt went on strike; then the postal workers, the social workers, the school-teachers, the clerical workers in the universities. Then the garbage collectors, the hospital staff, the farmers, eventually the buses and tubes and then the railways. It seemed as if war had been declared. When one remembers how completely hysterical the entire population of Britain becomes if there is an electricity strike which results in their having to plan their day around three hours' absence of electricity, it is amazing how phlegmatically the French population dealt with what must have seemed a far greater disaster. Although we now know the entire affair took place over about six weeks, at the time the newspaper headlines made it clear that there was no way of predicting an end. There was massive hoarding of food, as one didn't know whether fresh stocks would be in next week or at Christmas. Housewives with families to feed were more affected than us students, who ate erratically at the best of times and were high on too many other things to worry about food. The absence of petrol prevented mobility and emphasised a battle mentality. It made those of us who were in the centre of town feel, not as if we were under siege, but as if we had just seen one off and were triumphantly taking charge of the remains of our city. Remains it was: the streets of Paris in that pretty summer looked dismal: smoul-dering hulks of cars still left in the middle of the road, other cars which had not been destroyed, but whose owners had been too nervous to come back to reclaim them, vandalised and their tyres removed; many street signs torn down to add to the barricades, most of the trees along the Champs Elysées cut down for similar reasons; piles of garbage bags torn by cats and dogs during the night, with their contents rotting. There was such stillness – few cars moving, no buses or tubes, so few shops open that there were no shoppers (although the streets were beginning to fill with disaster-seeking tourists with cameras). That later period began to feel like a movie in slow motion in black and white, with all sound muffled and no sharpness of perception possible. There were so many unreal things. Not just the intensely interesting conversations of well-to-do parents discussing the revolutionary aspirations of their children. Not just the remarkably sulky withdrawal to Colombey-les-deux-Églises of de Gaulle, to whom some people were looking at that moment for a decisive act. I and a Dutch au pair girlfriend, who was fascinated and excited by all the running about and entirely uncomprehending of the issues, decided to take a night off from the revolution and go to a favourite dive in insalubrious Montmartre. We were quite furious to realise that there was no transport except our feet, to climb up those thigh-stretching hills and calf-burning steps!

By the end of the summer it looked as if the tumult was over, exhaustion had triumphed, the forces of order were again in control.

But in fact the control was nervous and wary, de Gaulle never did recover, and those who actually experienced the events went on to formulate their later political positions, with the anger, the excitement, the fear of the bullets, the sharpness of argument, the intense pleasure of sharing and support as part of their mental furniture.

In September 1968 a group of French women held a conference to discuss the lessons they could learn from their experience of the *événements*, the patronising attitude of their male colleagues, the difficulties of establishing feminist arguments on the agenda, the practical obstacles experienced by women students in playing as active a role as the men. That conference, followed by a second one the next spring, formed the origins of the French women's movement, predating the British by two years. English women are now just discovering the writers of this French movement and I think this is the richest inheritance of the Paris events that we have.

Of course the French government followed the example of governments everywhere when faced with rebellion among its citizenry, and blamed the trouble on unrest fermented artificially by foreigners who didn't have the well-being of French people at heart. The best way to distract attention from faults of government is an appeal to xenophobia. When my residence permit came up in September it was not renewed. I had to leave France, and it was many years before I could bring myself to go there again.

Sue O'Sullivan

My Old Man Said Follow
the Vanguard

It's beginning to feel odd and unsettling – all this looking
back, reflecting on the past. It makes it into an object to be
examined, one which is finished off, looked at through
barricades of years gone by. Then me today is severed from
me yesterday or else I'm a walking, talking relic. Positioning
myself in the 1960s goes against my emotional grain – not
mind you, that I don't get off on memories, on recording
events and feelings. It's just that now, at the end of the
eighties, it seems that instead of telling people we made
history at the beginning of the women's liberation movement,
I'm being told that I'm part of history.

I'm forty-six-years-old and can remember fiercely and

passionately saying to myself in 1969 that women's liberation was my life, would remain my life until I died. I might not be so fierce or passionate, the agenda is certainly different, but I still believe that I'll be involved in something more than a personal feminism until I die. Women's liberation is what enabled me to make sense of the world, enabled me to live with incomplete or contradictory answers, gave me an intellectual and emotional curiosity, sustained me and led me to develop faltering courage in myself and ultimately opened the door to lesbianism for me. The women's liberation movement, my participation in it, has been the means by which I've wiggled and wormed my way unevenly through the privileges, assumptions and constraints of my class, race and sex so that I sometimes live with what feels like a knowing engagement with politics.

The sixties were very much a bridging time, taking up of new identities and roles which had obvious connections to my life as a young girl and teenager in the fifties. In 1960 I turned nineteen and completed my first year of college. Neither I nor any of my friends took much notice of leaving the fifties. Perhaps you don't note dates so much at that age – you're so much *in* them that the transition from one decade to the next has no defined meaning. At the same time I felt that the fifties were mine, mine to feel attached to, formed by, trapped in – my youth. Elvis singing 'Heartbreak Hotel', The Penguins' 'Earth Angel', the fashions, the Korean War, pacifism, the fear and undercurrent I didn't really understand which was part of liberal/left politics, an unformed moral sense of the unjustness of prejudice . . . growing up liberal, white. Even now I get a *frisson* of irritation and amusement when fashion decrees the fifties are back – how could they want to bring that back, and anyway they've got it *all* wrong. As far as gender went, I didn't feel consciously rebellious about sex inequalities. I was preoccupied with the horror and injustice of killing, war, much affected by the Holocaust and fears of the atom bomb. Racial prejudice seemed cruel and wrong, I was naïvely righteous about it with no real conception of my own problematic place in the scheme of things.

I had no analysis of why bad things happened in the world,

or for that matter between people, except that they were wrong. I was reduced to frustrated, humiliated tears more than once while engaged in a tough argument with young sailors stationed at the submarine base not too far from my parents' rural Connecticut home. There on the sandy, summer beach, what would start out as a flirtation would end in impotent misery – I couldn't explain what I believed more than to defend it as morally right. Once at college there were encounters with more sophisticated cynical young men and women, who spouted cold war 'facts and figures' effectively against my 'soft' feelings. I was exposed and small and enraged – but I was never persuaded to drop my beliefs.

I almost made it into the sixties a virgin. But I'd been picked up and enthusiastically fucked by an 'older man' while visiting New York City for the first time during the week after graduating from high school. Classically, that first fuck was a huge let down. Dizzy and wet with desire, I'd abandoned my fears only to discover that I wasn't even sure 'it' had happened. A huge chasm opened up between my desires and my sexual practice. One which widened in the more permissive environment and times I found myself in at college in the early sixties.

As far as men or boys went we were a dismissive little bunch of heterosexual girls – but true to our times we put out for them even as we gossiped nastily behind their backs. We nicknamed one Greenwich Village man who dated a number of us 'Squirrel Monkey' because he crawled all over nibbling, and Ellen told us about her date, who when they were 'parking' late at night unzipped his fly and invited her to feel. 'Put that thing away', was her outraged command and the phrase entered our joking sexual vocabulary.

But we put out, either because we wanted to be in love or because it was too much trouble to say no. As opposed to sexual exploits, we didn't talk about sexual pleasure at all. I remember the bemused and confused response which greeted the revelation that Judith 'came' almost as soon as her boyfriend entered her. I'm amazed now when I think of the sexual acrobatics I performed back then with no pleasurable outcome – I could move my hips for hours, take it on all fours, fuck fast and furious, be on top, be stimulated by hand or mouth, grudgingly suck someone off and never a glimmer of the pleasure I felt in anticipation or in fantasy.

It was all a mystery to me – once after fucking for ages with my 'older man', who wasn't at all a wham-bam-thank-you-ma'am type, I felt my hands and feet tingling and asked my sophisticated lover if it could be an orgasm. He was quite sweet really and opined that I'd hyperventilated. The frustrating part of all this – and it involved about ten men over three years – was that I kept on desiring something, kept on getting wet and wanting it until it happened. And through it all I never used birth control.

In 1961 I came to London in search of a junior year abroad. I lived with two American college friends and never found a college that would accept me. The year was a significant one: chaotic, a little bit wild and for me a step away from my previous and predictable life.

I was away from my homeland, my parents, living independently from institutional structures, rules and provisions. I threw myself into dance classes at Madame de Vos' ballet studio in Notting Hill Gate where my modern training stuck out a mile. Martha Graham was practically unknown and London Contemporary Dance a long way off. I had no ballet training and in class would reduce myself to self-flagellating tears of frustration. But Madame de Vos liked me and together we'd watch advanced classes from the upstairs balcony where she would criticise certain rigidities in British training which left dancers unable to move their backs freely.

Otherwise I hung around coffee bars or the LSE graduate lounge where my friends and I had made acquaintances. There I met a young man I fell head over heels in love with and right before my return to the States, I had my first ever orgasm with him. But before coming for the first time, I came in contact with people whose political perspectives and cultures were completely different from mine. They spoke to my concerns and confidently answered many of the arguments I'd engaged in so ineffectively in the USA. Socialism wasn't a dirty word. Here I encountered class for the first time. As is still true for the majority of Americans, I had no knowledge

116

of class as either an historical heritage or as part of a political analysis. I'd never been taught anything about the rich and varied American class struggles of the nineteenth and twentieth centuries. My grandfather had been a 'poor boy' who 'worked his way up'. To talk about class smacked of communism and even for many liberals and/or poor people that was anathema. The young man I fell in love with was a socialist, a Marxist even. His father was in the Communist Party and his whole family was poor, radical and working class.

After that year in London I spent a year back in the USA longing to get back to London and I made it clear to my parents that come hell or high water, that's where I was going. For once I felt completely confident that I wanted to throw my lot in with someone else – there were no questions or hesitations. I knew that John didn't believe in marriage, I didn't think I did, but I managed to convince myself and him that we should – for my parents' sake. I doubt that was the whole story. I think I wanted to get married, even if I flippantly said to my best friend in the USA 'Oh, you can always get divorced', shortly before taking the marriage plunge.

After college finished for the year, I got the first Icelandic flight to London I could and winged my way back to freedom and love.

The sixties for me was leaving my parents' home in order to set up one with my husband. I'd been away at school and college for years but 'home' was still with the family, and with the exception of my year in London when I lived with two friends, I'd never been remotely near to living on my own. I would be forty-one years old before I did so. The sixties years were about separating myself from the USA and everything I couldn't get to grips with there – and an important part of that was the benign but controlling influence of my parents. It was a time to develop my independence and to take shaky steps towards a politics which wasn't based primarily on moral outrage. For me, it happened within a marriage which challenged many of the middle-class assumptions and patterns of my parents' and contemporaries' marriages. We were not part of 'swinging London': although I thought about the

117

constraints of monogamy from time to time, in day to day terms it simply wasn't an issue. We were both monogamous and with the exception of one or two little fantasies about particular men, I never fancied or slept with another man.

Although I didn't find monogamous marriage sexually restrictive, still off and on I felt the terrible absence of my friends. I'd always had close and constant girlfriends – boyfriends and lovers might come and go, but we girls were loyal and committed to each other. I met my best friend when I was six and had a number of other women friends from high school. But come marriage or 'living together' and we went our separate ways. There was nothing I knew then which might have enabled me to conceptualise this mutual and accepted abandonment.

During the year I was back in the USA, away from but in love with John, I had an illegal abortion. A few minutes passively participating in a lonely, drunken, joyless fuck led to a secret, dazed Puerto Rican abortion on Valentine's eve. There was absolutely no question in my mind about that abortion. I 'knew' I was pregnant immediately but I never thought of the foetus as a baby. My search for an abortion and for the money to pay for it left me exhausted – the underground of illegal abortions was a nightmare. I was lucky to find a proper, if squalid, money spinning clinic; friends were not so fortunate and endured abortions in abandoned New York city tenements, lying on newspaper on the floor with a bottle of whisky to dull the pain, being left alone to struggle to the street when it was over and make their way home. Others made assignments with male voices on the phone, directed to highway exit telephone booths where they were then sent on to a second pickup point to finally pay for the chemicals they were to drink. These were supposed to bring on a miscarriage which would have to be finished off in a hospital where the woman was warned she would risk arrest if she breathed a word of how she happened to be mis-carrying.

In my search I was supported and helped by my close women friends at college. One day a friend borrowed a car and four of us set off for upstate New York where someone had heard there was a well known abortionist. Arriving in the little town, we somehow managed to make our way to the address, only to find that the man was 'away'. His assistant proceeded to examine me in what I realised half-way through was a purely sexual way. He had no intention of giving me an abortion. Deflated, disgusted and frantic, I was at least surrounded by the care and concern of my friends. The Puerto Rican connection came through a New York man I had dated but had no desire to sleep with. The night before flying there I spent in the city with him. I was doing what I desperately wanted to do but was in a state of blanked-out emotions. That night, the bastard who was 'helping' me fucked me, and I went through it as if in a dream; it seemed part of the payment I had to make.

My search for an abortion and for the money went on side by side with the necessity of maintaining a normal façade and carrying on as usual. I took exams, performed in a series of dance recitals and gave nothing away. My girlfriends took me through it all and a room-mate's mother spontaneously lent me the bulk of the money I needed. Six months later when I sent her the first repayment, she wrote back to tell me that she didn't want the money back, that she had had an abortion as a young woman and understood my situation. If the time came when I was older and had more money, she hoped I would help another young woman out. These were the sorts of friends I was leaving, but with hugs and promises to write, and with thoughts only on England, I flew off.

I was terrified of telling John about my abortion – away from my true love for a year and look what happens! I was afraid he would reject me – not so much for the abortion but because I slept with someone else. He was hurt and I hated that, but he accepted it and never used it against me.

In London we lived on John's grant, supplemented by his occasional supply teaching and some gifts from my parents. I didn't worry about working as long as we were getting by. I wanted to dance but there was no way I could earn a living at it. Teaching was not on as I didn't have a degree. John was accustomed to being poor and I experienced living without the middle-class comforts of American life as liberating. I was part of a generation of Americans who were questioning a conservative consumer-oriented society, so living without a fridge, vacuum cleaner, TV or central heating didn't bother me a bit. (Now I can see the inverted class dimensions of the ease with which I accepted less than I had been used to, but I'm still glad I went that way.) We spent what money we had on going to films at the National Film Theatre, plays at the Royal Court and occasional meals at Jimmy's or our local Indian restaurant. I didn't drink or at that point smoke. We were childless. We revelled in our tiny basement flat. Certainly my middle-class background informed the relief I experienced stepping out of those particular class expectations.

After two years' married life in Camden Town, when I took up dance classes at Madame de Vos' again, typed my husband's PHD thesis, tried to learn how to cook, and socialised mainly with John's friends, we decided to spend a year in the USA so I could finish my college degree.

We ended up staying for two years in New York City. Being back in the USA, married and living in a small rent-controlled flat in Greenwich Village during the mid-sixties turned out to be an exciting and different experience for both of us. John got his first teaching job at the New School for Social Research, at that time a left haven in American academia, and he stepped right into the middle of New Left activism and renewed interest in Marxism. Many of his students, not much younger that he was, were involved in Students for a Democratic Society (SDS) and a number of them became close and lasting friends. Being involved in left-wing politics at that point meant anti-Vietnam war work, community politics and the challenge of Black Power.

This was mostly John's terrain. I cared deeply about the issues, and my ideas were influenced, particularly about racism, but I didn't feel part of the student world and wasn't sure where I fitted in. Many of my friends had been involved in the civil rights movement during the two years I was in England and I had followed it in the news and radical press. Back in the States, I personally experienced the strength of the anti-war movement, the necessity to stand up and be counted right there in the 'belly of the monster'. Anti-war demonstrations in New York city drew in such a huge cross-section of pacifists, radicals and militant Black people, plus many previously uninvolved 'ordinary citizens' that it took my breath away, and more than once I was moved to tears. But I continued to go along to demonstrations as an individual, still carrying with me a very American reluctance to subsume an idealised individuality into any notion of a collective.

I didn't agonise over any of this too much. I was busy commuting daily to college, dancing and just getting a buzz out of living in the city. When friends came over at night, the conversation would be of politics: class, Marxism, the war, organising, SDS, racism, consumerism, American capitalism. I wasn't bored at all, but I tended to feel that I was listening-in and I knew that the men, no matter how nice, weren't particularly interested in my or the other women's lives. I remember one conversation between two of us women about the side effects of the Pill – did it give us headaches or weight gain? We carried on for a while with the men making little additions to the conversation. I remember it well because it was unusual for women to dominate the conversation with 'woman talk'. However there was no undercurrent of resentment and we certainly didn't complain. When John and I got together with my school and college friends, the women dominated the conversation as much as the men. It wasn't that the women I knew had nothing to say, only that we, as much as the men, tended to accept that some areas of conversation and concern were more the men's. No one ever articulated this and therefore it was never a topic of speculation or debate.

The second year in New York city both John and I worked and for the first time had money to spare. We ate bagels with cream cheese, onion and smoked salmon at a 6th Avenue luncheonette, frequented a tiny Italian restaurant south of Houston Street in what is now trendy SoHo but was then an old Italian neighbourhood. We attended dance concerts around the City, saw all the radical theatre going, bought the Sunday *New York Times* late on Saturday nights, nipping home to pull out the fold-up bed and settle in for a luxurious read. I bought dozens of cheap earrings at the Jewel Box on 8th Street and blew my first pay cheque on a fur bedspread. We saw Bo Diddley and other musicians at local venues and with a group of SDS friends travelled up town to the big 'Be In' in Central Park. I never thought of myself as a hippy and now I have to laugh when my boys call me one. I stayed away from long print skirts and ran a mile at the idea of 'love beads', being much more attracted to an earlier bohemian image.

Living in the city for two years had a profound effect on John: he was welcomed into left intellectual groupings, and felt less an interloper in the looser American academic scene than in the more rigidly class-stratified British one. The vitality and dedication with which people on the left were engaging with politics excited him; his Marxism and class-consciousness made him a valuable part of these groups.

For me the years were significant for other reasons. I enjoyed the easy socialising with old and new friends and immersed myself in the city's culture, seeing it all anew after living in London for two years. I'd never lived in the States as an 'adult', nor had I lived before in an American city. I'd finished my degree successfully, getting more out of that final year as a 'mature' student than ever before. I had a job and time to take dance classes at the Merce Cunningham Studio which I loved. As happy and productive as that time was, it was a temporary sojourn; we both wanted to return to London.

In the early spring of 1967 when we'd already decided to return to London that summer, John suggested we have a baby and I thought, 'Hey, why not?' I never doubted I'd have kids some day and we'd already been married for four years. I didn't dwell much on what it would mean. I assumed I would be okay as a mother. After all, from the age of eleven I'd enjoyed an ace reputation as a babysitter, I'd been a successful nursery teacher – I loved kids. Anyway ever since high school everyone told me I'd be a great mother.

In early summer 1967 we packed bits of furniture and belongings in wooden crates and clutching carrier bags with kitchen utensils poking out the top we flew back to London, me just pregnant. My pregnancy was spent in Stoke Newington in London where we finally found a flat. No more cheap central London basement flats we could afford. Until I was about six or seven months pregnant, I trekked across London to go to dance classes. One day Madame de Vos took me aside and explained apologetically that I would have to stop classes. A rather large pregnant woman leaping around was making the other students nervous. A few years earlier a teacher of mine had taught an energetic class the day before she gave birth. Ah well, this was England and I stopped. I felt more and more lonely and isolated. I didn't know anyone where I lived, transportation was poor and no one dropped by. I felt acutely, for the first time since I married, the absence of friends. I wobbled a bit.

John had found a university teaching job and was involved in teacher/student politics. I went on anti-Vietnam war demonstrations, keeping well to the side at Grosvenor Square, accompanied John to political meetings, and started natural birth classes at Charing Cross Hospital. I practised my breathing exercises religiously. My mother had been knocked out when giving birth to all three of her children and I had decided that I wanted to be fully awake and 'in control'. The teacher advised women to open their mouths wide in the final stages of delivery, as the vagina would follow suit. She had given this advice to her own daughter before her wedding night and was sure that it helped! This titbit of information was imparted to us at a 'fathers' night' and a white South African Communist I'd met there, her husband, John and I sat at the back of the room like naughty schoolkids choking back our laughter.

I didn't laugh much in labour. I was late and huge. One morning I got out of the bed which took up most of the room. I stood naked in front of the full length mirror on the wardrobe, looked at myself and shrieked. Literally overnight my belly was rippled with stretch marks. Baby was outgrowing the womb. A few days later I went into hospital with high blood pressure and for days lay around miserably while different doctors decided first to induce, then to wait, then to induce, until I finally started of my own accord.

It went on and on and on. I was picked up and tossed into labour. I was out of control. I hung on to my breathing like a shipwrecked thing until the labour went into chaos. This was not anything like the books or the teacher said, where the anarchy of the transitional phase lasts a relatively short time. I was vomiting, hooked up to a drip, exhausted and thought I might die. After being knocked out with an injection for a few hours, I woke up only to have it all start again at the same stage. After more than thirty hours in labour they wheeled me into the delivery room – 'Time to push, mother'. This was not a great success and I ended up with deep forceps thrust in me in order to haul an over-nine-pound, traumatised baby into the world. I lay there, bloody, bowed and blank. All I wanted to do was sleep. (When he was about two, Tom claimed he could remember the struggle to be born.)

John fell in love hook line and sinker the moment he held Tom. I went into a lengthy period of subdued shock. My breasts filled up to bursting with milk and I had to go on a monstrous milking machine to express the extra to feed ailing babies. I was the breast-feeding star of the ward. Sisters went from bed to bed coaxing reluctant nipples into recalcitrant babies' mouths. Women who were desperately keen to breast-feed had problems, women who didn't want to were bullied into it. My breasts squirted, my baby sucked heartily from the first.

But my cunt was a misery. I could hardly make it down the hall to the loo. I felt like my insides would burst out the minute I stood up; sitting down was agony and only possible on a foam rubber ring. I couldn't believe this was normal but everyone said it was. Months later in the USA a friend's doctor husband had a look because I was still in so much pain. He said I'd been sewed up badly and unevenly after the episiotomy.

Back in Stoke Newington I sat with my big, quiet, wide-eyed baby and stared at him wondering who I was, who he was. I sat for hours with him on the breast, I wiped up shit, pinned nappies on, lay on the floor trying to figure out where the muscles were which would allow me to attempt sit-ups and wondered. I was floundering badly but I think I must have looked all right. Pictures from my album show smiling or contemplative family life. There *was* pleasure and contentment, but through it all I felt displaced emotionally. I wasn't sure what anything meant. I'd joined the grown-up world of mothers and yet I felt more unsure and lonely than ever before. I could perform all the techniques of motherhood competently, I was riveted by the baby, but I had an awful feeling that being a mother didn't fit me well. I was a failure in what I assumed would come most naturally. I had seen myself at best as happy and flexible, not dependent on a baby to give my life meaning, welcoming it rather as a new dimension of responsibility and pleasure. That the experience was different from what I'd imagined it would be wouldn't necessarily have been depressing as I quite liked being taken by surprise, startled and then coming to grips with new feelings and circumstances. No, this was something different and much more fundamentally fearful and guilt-inspiring.

I heard about women's liberation the first summer I was a mother and paid it no special heed. It was 1968, students were in revolt, the Chinese Cultural Revolution was in full tilt, we were told there'd been a sexual revolution. I myself had participated in CND marches and anti-war demonstrations, I'd had an abortion, moved continents, married, finished a degree, worked and had a baby. As the decade moved to a close I came undone. I regretted none of it, but could see no coherency in my life. I was married and now had another man's name; I had a baby and was therefore a mother. I'd been taught to value myself as an individual at the same time that selfishness was castigated. I'd been encouraged to get a liberal education and broaden my horizons, but with no particular goal in mind other than being a better human being. My personal feelings of outrage at injustice had been nurtured but I couldn't find a way into sustained activity for meaningful change. I was ripe for women's liberation but had to make the connection for myself.

In 1969 I went along to a small women's group in Tufnell Park. Twenty years later I'm still involved, in a very different way, in women's liberation, although it's not even called that anymore. I had another baby in March 1970, a week after attending the first women's liberation conference at Ruskin College in Oxford. I went with John and Tom. All the women I knew were heterosexual and many had small children. We all believed that women's liberation would create better relationships between men and women. I still believe that's ultimately true, but what none of us could contemplate at that moment was how profoundly it might shake up our own relationships with men.

Is it mainly men of my generation who are nostalgic about the sixties? Certainly for me, it's the seventies which signal change, growth and understanding of things. It was in the seventies that I became part of a movement which made sense of the world in a way which also gave me agency. I can wax nostalgic about aspects of sixties culture and be moved all over again by the struggles which other oppressed groups waged. I can see the connections and acknowledge my debt to those. But it's the world-wide revolt of women in the seventies which ushered me so firmly into a politics which encompassed the public and the personal, with all the attendant pleasures and pains which that implies.

LIVING

··

'Doing what comes naturally'

Michelene Wandor

In the Sixties

in the sixties, I
left home
got a degree
got married
had two children
separated
started writing
became a feminist
became a socialist

in the sixties, I
wore very, very, very short mini-skirts
tried to sit carefully, so as not to show my knickers
wore lots of mascara
worried that my nose would shine red through my make-up
    (which it did) when I had a cold (which was often)
was told I 'had the best legs in London'
learned to jive
was very snooty about the early Beatles
got hooked on Buddy Holly and the Everly Brothers
wore contact lenses

in the sixties, I
was terrified of the world outside my home
couldn't wait to leave home
was terrified of the world outside University
fell in love

in the sixties, I
was the first girl from my (mixed) grammar school to be at (go
    up to) Cambridge University
in the sixties I first felt the shock of not having the right
    accent or enough money
in the sixties I was going to be Sarah Bernhardt (with two
    legs)
in the sixties I found it very hard to sit still in libraries
in the sixties I packed plastic potties in my summer holidays
    (sorry, vacations)
in the sixties I delivered the post at Christmas
in the sixties I fell in love with oh so many desirable people of
    all possible sexes and did nothing (conscious) about it

in sixties' Cambridge
I acted in dozens of plays
directed one
loved the buildings
was upset by the snobbery
met people who are still friends
met people who are now famous
for the first time ever met people whose parents were

divorced and was amazed to find they were still whole
people
played the recorder secretly and very fast in my college room
played the clarinet publicly and was never happy with my
embouchure

in sixties' Cambridge
I fell in love for absolutely real
and lots of things were done about it
most of them wonderful
and some of them appalling

in the sixties, I
tried hard to be a good wife and mother (honest)
cooked from Carrier, Deighton and David (still got the books
to prove it)
had a Mary Quant haircut
wore hand-me-down Biba dresses swapped for books with
one of the girls who worked there
entertained George Steiner and Anthony Burgess to dinner,
followed by Jean Shrimpton and Heathcote Williams (to
name but a few)

in the sixties, you see, I
was the wife of an up-and-coming young publishing executive
we went to parties; despite having top-notch educational
credentials, I still had the wrong accent and was 'just' a
housewife
in the sixties I was, as I was in the forties, fifties, seventies and
eighties, the daughter of Jewish Polish-Russian immigrants

so

in the sixties, I
fell in love seriously twice more, with my sons Adam and Ivan
in the sixties, I
began to discover that the love affair you have with your
children lasts forever

in the sixties, I
went to see the Living Theatre at the Round House and La
Mama in Notting Hill

in the sixties, I
met Richard and Louise and Marsha and the *Oz* lot and
    thought they were something else, and went to UFO and
    dazzled mine eyes on graphic magazines and saw my first
    pornographic film, and envied people who slept around a
    lot and wondered how they did it and never found out, but
    then I was still 'just' a housewife, albeit with the 'best legs in
    London', though Louise's were pretty hot competition, I
    must say

in the sixties, I
lusted over more legs than you've had hot dinners

in the sixties, I
tried to smoke pot (man) but couldn't because I have asthma
    and couldn't inhale the smoke

in the sixties, I
had a hot line in hash fudge, courtesy of the corruption of a
    recipe from Florence Greenberg's Jewish Cookery Book (I
    bet she'd never heard of Alice B. Toklas)
in the sixties, I
finally learned to love the psychedelic Beatles
finally learned to use Tampax
tried the pill, the coil and the cap (God, what a drag)
visited my parents regularly every week and shouted at my
    father (he shouted first, honest)

in the sixties, I
was ill a lot
stopped playing the recorder
had never heard of the viol

the sixties
were full of people I didn't sleep with
joints I didn't smoke
plays I wasn't in

the sixties were
when everything
and everyone
got stirred up

the sixties
were full
of unrequited lusts

the sixties was a time when many people went to pot
except for me
I did not

during the sixties
I yearned
a lot

Lee Kane

Including Me?

There is a lot of nostalgia about the sixties. Portrayed by the media as the era of the 'love and peace generation', of free love, free pop concerts, the Beatles and LSD, it is fondly recalled as a time when we were on the verge of creating a new society. 'Times they are a-changing', sang Dylan, as the new generation challenged the old morality, ridiculed accepted values, and dismissed established institutions. It was the era of protest. In Britain there was a mass movement against nuclear weapons and war. This pacifist movement gave way to the more militant Vietnam Solidarity campaign and the violent demonstrations in Grosvenor Square. The Labour Party was returned to power in 1964, after thirteen years of Conservative rule, and for a brief time people believed that socialism had arrived. In the colleges, student protest rumbled on, reaching a crescendo in 1968, not only in Britain, but internationally.

My feelings about the sixties are mixed. This is the era which gave birth to many movements which have influenced me. Civil rights in America gave birth to Black power. The political movements of the sixties necessitated the women's movement of the seventies. Many of us developed through CND to a commitment to anti-imperialist struggles. Involvement in the Labour Party and its fate when in power, taught us to examine more closely who holds the reins. Nevertheless this time was unreal for me, because like millions of others, I was more an observer than a participant. I was a weekend hippy, who conformed for the rest of the week. I was a would-be revolutionary, who was refused admission to the revolution because I did not have the entry qualifications. This was because it took place mainly in the colleges and universities, in isolation from the rest of the population, whose attitude to students varied from indifference to contempt.

I personally did not find the sixties liberating. In 1960, I was sixteen. My father had just died and I was living with my mother, who was becoming increasingly depressive. I was attending a Catholic school, by which, despite my resistance, I had been partially conditioned. School was a very negative experience. They had already told me that they did not expect me to pass exams because I did not have the culture to do so. This was particularly ironic since my parents had chosen the school to protect me from being damaged by racism. Apart from being racist, the school was riddled with snobbery, the nuns were vicious (most unlike *The Nun's Story*) and the education was of an extremely low standard. The nuns expected little of most of the girls. Marriage was to be our main priority, and childbirth, though we were given little advice about this except it was implied that we were to keep ourselves pure and not be flighty. A few of us might be clever enough to go to college first.

In 1964, I had fulfilled the first part of the school's educational dream for me, though not exactly as intended. I got married. By 1970, I was pregnant with my second child, and shortly to be separated. In those ten years many of my attitudes had changed fundamentally. By 1970, I was beginning to question my romantic view of marriage and beginning to see what had happened and was happening to me as an individual and in my private life in a new light.

My life has been full of contradictions. I went to a private school, although my parents were not rich. They both worked, at a time when many women stayed at home. My mother was an office worker and my father a stoker. Neither had had much education. My dad was illiterate, and my mum left school after elementary education. Because of this they both prized education, and thought, wrongly as it turned out, that it must be good if you pay for it. They were both intimidated by the school and avoided contact with it once I went, and knew little about what I was taught. School life and home life were kept well apart. We lived in a battered, privately-rented house, which backed on to the railway. The house was multi-occupied and we had two rooms at first. Fortunately somebody died and we gained two more, when I was about thirteen. There were no facilities. We put in our own electricity, hot water and kitchen sink. The other tenants had gaslight and we all shared the toilet. Our conditions were so bad that, by tacit agreement, school friends were not invited to my home. Apart from my family, our only visitors were neighbourhood friends whose situation was the same as ours. Even so, most people kept themselves to themselves, which in the circumstances seemed the best way to deal with the situation.

At one stage I used to suggest that we should look for better housing. My parents made it clear that this would not be possible. Although they never spelt it out exactly I soon gathered that this was because of racism. Their legacy to me was a strange one. They wanted me to succeed and did not seem to appreciate that there might be obstacles. Each of them hinted at the difficulties they had faced in their own lives. My dad was fiercely proud of all things Black, and from him I learned about conditions in South Africa, his home country. My mum was a protagonist of women's rights. But by the time I reached adolescence, any fire they may once have possessed was weakened.

Although I stayed on at school until I was eighteen, I was very glad to leave. In my head I rejected religion, trembling in case God heard me, and withdrew myself from school as often as possible. On one occasion, however, I organised a petition to the Colonial Office. In the sixth form we were regularly treated to lectures from visiting anti-communists. One such visitor, a nun from a mission in Belize, aroused my sympathy for the plight of the people, who had suffered a major disaster aggravating, she said, their existing poverty. We had been asked to organise a collection to provide blankets. I volunteered, but half-way through the collection it occurred to me that if the people were suffering this must be the responsibility of colonialism. So instead of sending donations to the Colonial Office as requested I sent a letter of protest. My action and views were naïve, but it was a beginning.

The company I was beginning to mix with was a refreshing change from the values of the convent. It was also different from my peers in the neighbourhood, who were all thinking about and getting married. For most of them this was the only way of leaving home but it also appeared to be an unspoken rule that if you slept with someone you married them. My new group was cynical, proud of their lowly origins, mentioned other cultures with respect and talked about the international solidarity of the working class. I met a wide range of people, from all parts of Britain and from abroad. There was an active social life, and for the first time I appeared to be dealing with people on equal terms who did not try to excuse the fact that I was Black. I did outrageous things, attending CND marches, rallies etc, sleeping out in dubious circumstances in mixed company and attending all-night parties. In reality much of the activity was tame. I, at any rate, remained extremely conservative and the main reason I was out all night was because the buses had stopped running and I couldn't get home. My mother was not amused; although she did not interfere she did make me feel guilty.

Politics met a social need but it also offered an explanation for the racism which I had encountered and the conditions in which I lived. I learned that poor housing and poverty were not caused by individual failure; I was told that racism was a deliberate ploy, capitalism's attempt to divide the working class. Although later I found this explanation too simplistic, because it ignored our experience of racism, it helped me take the first step towards understanding how society shapes our destiny. I was, however, still an observer. I attended various meetings, at first on my own and then accompanying my boyfriend. I overheard rather than participated in debates. I sat through hours of discussion without voicing one political thought. I was not alone. Hardly any of the women spoke. Those who did were viewed with a mixture of awe and disdain.

When I was 20 my mother died. I got married for a mixture of reasons. I thought I was in love. I was due to start college away from home. I was scared of having nobody, did not want to go to a new town alone and was reluctant to end a relationship which I had already tried to end before. He was supportive. We seemed to understand and need each other. Anyway we hedged our bets. We married in a hurry but in the understanding that marriage was no big deal. If we didn't like it we could get a divorce. In a strange way, despite the fact that we had no money, I found marriage liberating at first. Since I belonged to someone I felt released to relate more easily to people in general, but to men in particular. The conventions of marriage, of male chauvinism, relieved me from having to consider whether men might misread the situation, or whether I was placing myself in a vulnerable position. My self-confidence increased. I no longer had to fear being left on the shelf. I could give my personality free rein and get on with pursuing my own interests. I did not, however, seriously consider what sort of relationship we had or wanted.

After two years in Coventry we returned to London, to the house that I had lived in with my parents for a while, then we were rehoused. I found work and for the first time began to participate politically of my own volition. I began to get involved with issues and campaigns which I could identify with, like housing, racial discrimination, claimants, etc. I was beginning, however, to feel constricted by marriage. I was a fairly traditional wife, although nominally we believed in equality, women working rather than being at home. At this stage, however, the feeling was vague. If I thought about the possibility of being married to the same person for forty years it filled me with dread. Generally I did not think about it. I began to notice, though, that many of my friends who now had children were consigned to a secondary role. Their husbands rarely discussed anything with them, were often out and generally abandoned them at home whilst they socialised in the pub, or undertook politically significant tasks.

I was not particularly sympathetic, having not yet had children myself. I concentrated my energies on ensuring that I would not be abandoned with the mothers. There was little question of sisterly solidarity. I sought to participate with the men, though not always successfully. Their conversations were aimed at each other. In 1968, my first child was born. He was a wanted child, but his birth ensured my dependence. I could not go out unless baby-sitting was arranged. Finances were very tight, and I returned to work part-time shortly after he was born, feeling guilty. Ours was not a co-operative parenthood. The responsibility for his care was all mine. I was tired, and began to feel bored and boring. In contrast the world outside was erupting. The student revolution was about to change the world. Into what was questionable, since neither women nor Black people seemed essential to that struggle. In the meantime I was on the verge of discovering that the personal is political, that as Black people we too have a history, and that liberation included me. How these strands would come together is another story.

Patricia Vereker

From Emancipation to
Liberation

There was a gap of about twenty-five years, as well as World
War II, between my adolescence and my children's 'teenage'
years in the sixties. There are inevitable changes in such a
period of time, but the upheaval of the war caused these
changes to occur more rapidly. After the war, however, there
seemed to be a desire to return to normal life, and 'normal'
meant life as it had been in the past. I do not think I became
fully aware of the impact of the changes until my children
became 'teenagers', when I was obliged to confront the world
in which they were growing up, which appeared to be very
different in so many ways from the world of my own
adolescence.

It seems now that I grew up at a time when life was less
complicated for young people in that there were fewer
choices; the rules of accepted behaviour were clearer, even if
not always obeyed, or obeyed through fear rather than
freedom of choice. The problems of adolescence were much
the same but were barely spoken of and little allowance was
made for moods or rebellion. I was at school in the aftermath
of the suffragette movement, yet I took the vote for granted,
even though universal suffrage for all over twenty-one did
not take place until 1929. Our teachers told us that the whole
world was now open to women, we were emancipated, we
could follow any career we chose. I never noticed the signifi-

cance of the word 'emancipation'. I was educated in the same way as my brother, and my father was equally concerned that I should have a career. I saw women as the same as men except that, on the whole, they did different things; there was a division of labour and men and women were complementary. I never felt I was threatened by men, even though as an undergraduate reading law there were only three women in my year to about 150 men. Perhaps it would all have been different if I had tested my position in the market-place.

I do not remember talking about the position of women with any of my friends, although we had passionate discussions on political issues. None of our teachers drew our attention to the early feminist writers or to J. S. Mill, or even to *A Room of One's Own*. We learned about Florence Nightingale, Octavia Hill, Nurse Cavell and of course, Miss Buss and Miss Beale, but nothing about the suffragettes. The argument about the position of women was over, the battle was won. Perhaps I led a very sheltered life, or perhaps I lacked curiosity. My sense of equality was such that when I first read Betty Friedan's *The Feminine Mystique* I had no idea what she was writing about. It had nothing to do with me and I dismissed it as being American.

This was the history I brought with me when I faced the upbringing of my children in the changed world of greater freedom in sexual relations, the Pill, the student revolution and women's liberation.

I think what first struck me in the late fifties and early sixties was what appeared to be the sudden emergence of a distinctive group called 'teenagers' and that my own children were part of this group. While we had passed with as little attention as possible from childhood to adult life, there was now a well-publicised body of teenage needs, catered for by special clothes, make-up and magazines. Young people wanted more freedom to control their own lives and make their own decisions from a much earlier age. There was more openness about sexual relationships, paralleled by a demand for more information.

My memory is that in my time relationships between boys and girls were, on the whole, carefully regulated, and in any case were not of much concern until sixteen or seventeen. We were officially kept in ignorance of sex, a word which was rarely mentioned, except with bravado in groups of giggling schoolgirls who gathered in knots during break to share their garbled and inaccurate versions of the 'facts of life'. Biology lessons included the facts of reproduction up to but not including human reproduction. The phrase 'pre-marital intercourse' did not exist in our conversation but we all knew it was strictly forbidden because of the terrible fear of having an illegitimate baby. We knew little about contraceptives or where they could be obtained. Abortions were illegal, and back-street abortions, which we did know about, were dangerous and expensive. We also knew that if we did get pregnant we would be disowned by our family and an outcast in society.

As my daughters approached their 'teens' I felt I had little experience from my childhood to draw on which would be useful in the very different situation of the sixties. In such trivial matters as what clothes, nylons, make-up and jewellery were appropriate at what age, I soon realised this was a lost cause in the face of group pressures and advertisers. I did intermittently enquire why it was necessary to be the same as everyone else, but I did not get very far with this line of questioning. Many conversations with friends about our children concerned the time we expected them to come home at night; this was a source of endless family argument, again with group pressure set against what we believed to be our better judgement. Again, we wondered whether children could be allowed to have parties at home without parents present. We discussed our views on pre-marital sex and were mostly firmly of the opinion that it was unwise, but our views were challenged by arguments we had not previously considered. Would it not be acceptable between two people who were committed to each other even though they were not married? What was wrong with it provided you were careful? How could you commit yourself to marriage for life without making sure beforehand that you enjoyed sex together? Later, when children had left home and you knew they were sleeping with their boyfriends or girlfriends, did you offer them a double bed when they came home together for the weekend? We had answers to these questions but we were uneasy and were never quite sure we had reached the right decision.

Each generation of parents must find similar difficulties because of the passage of time. I think that, perhaps, my generation found it particularly difficult because in the intervening years the prevailing psychology relating to childcare had become child-centred. Although I never discussed it with them, I am sure that my parents' generation had no doubt that they knew what was best for their children, whereas we were filled with doubts. I was first struck by the change in childcare when I witnessed demand feeding – 'Baby knows best'. The book[1] I used on the care of young babies, first published in 1940 and reprinted every year until 1945, if not later, said 'most babies do best if fed four-hourly; the most convenient times being 6.0am, 10.0am, 2.0pm, 6.0pm and 10.0pm . . . as a rule no night feed is given . . . But there are babies who cannot go through the 8 hours wait and a feed at 2.0am may be necessary for a week or two.' I assume that these times were considered to be the most convenient for mothers. School teaching followed a similar direction and classes were child-led, working to the speed of the child and responding to the child's interests. All this was very new to us.

In 1960 I became involved with the Marriage Guidance Council's initiative for Education in Personal Relationships in schools and youth clubs, which put me in touch with a wide variety of young people and the questions they were asking. It also enlarged my experience of the problems faced by people of my generation in coming to terms with a changed world. The Marriage Guidance Council was responding to the anxieties of parents and teachers aroused by the greater freedom in relations between girls and boys and the greater openness in discussion of sexual matters in the press and on television, and among young people themselves. Biology lessons in schools still described reproduction in amoebas and frogs but did not include human reproduction. If human reproduction were to be included in the syllabus, there were many teachers, like parents, who had no experience of discussing these matters with the young. There was also a

143

further anxiety that if pupils were told all about human reproduction they might try it out for themselves. We feared that without the constraints within which we had grown up there would be an enormous increase in illegitimate babies, an increase in sexually transmitted disease and the breakdown of marriage and family life. The widespread attitude was reminiscent of the Victorian attitude to small children: 'Find out what baby is doing and tell him not to.' The Marriage Guidance Council's view was that sex education should take place within the context of marriage and family life. Adolescents should be treated as on their way to adulthood; they should be fully informed of the physical facts as well as the emotional and moral implications so that they could learn to make reasoned choices. Underlying this approach was clearly the hope that the choices would correspond to what we then believed was appropriate behaviour.

Marriage Guidance offered small informal discussion groups in schools and youth clubs for young people of about thirteen years of age upwards. Volunteers were carefully selected and trained to act as group leaders; they were to be men and women who were able to make easy contact with the young, open-minded, non-judgemental and not embarrassed by discussion of these intimate matters. The informal groups were intended to create a relaxed atmosphere in which young people would feel able to ask any questions and discuss between themselves and with the group leader their attitudes to relationships with the 'opposite sex', a phrase which I think is no longer in use. The guidelines were relatively clear. The groups were to be told the 'facts of life', which was the current euphemism for the facts of human reproduction. (I do not think this phrase is often used now; I have recently seen it referred to as 'plumbing'.) Discussion of sexual intercourse (you did not 'have sex' in those days) was to be placed firmly within a loving relationship, preferably within marriage, but at the very least with someone you knew well and to whom you were committed. There was less clarity about the topics which could or should be raised in the groups. There was endless discussion and much agonising about such subjects as contraceptives, abortion, homosexuality and masturbation, these last two referring only to men. It was very much a question of 'teacher educate yourself'. Looking back, I think it may have been the group leaders themselves who benefited most from having to confront the views with which they were brought up and being obliged to consider how far they were still appropriate.

The response from head teachers and youth club leaders was positive and welcoming. They saw that education in personal relationships ought to be 'done' in schools, and in youth clubs for an older age-group, but there were few who were willing to undertake it. There was also a feeling that it was better undertaken by a stranger to the group, although this changed later when teachers decided they would prefer to talk to their own pupils and some Local Education Authorities organised courses for selected teachers in their schools. I am not sure that the expectations of head teachers and youth club leaders were always met by the Marriage Guidance approach. There was some disapproval of informal discussion groups for such serious subject-matter. I was sometimes instructed before a session 'to be sure to tell the group what they ought to know', which meant no sex before marriage.

The response from the groups was, on the whole, enthusiastic. They appeared to be glad of the opportunity to ask questions, knowing these questions would be answered, in an area where they had so often met prevarication or silence. They even seemed pleased to be given what was then known as an acceptable vocabulary for parts of the body. As far as I remember, no four letter words were ever used. Some groups began by being reticent about asking questions, so they wrote them down for the group leader to read out anonymously. I cherish the memory of a number of written questions about 'sexual intercoarse'; and one from a Church youth club: 'Is it all right to have that which is intended inside marriage outside marriage or is the cost too great?' Most groups came to ask their own questions; factual questions were answered, and young people soon gained confidence to contribute their own views on questions of behaviour and they were encouraged to look at all sides of the question. If asked, the group leaders would give their own views, but only as one view among others. Many of the questions were much the same as parents were asking themselves. 'What time should I be home at night?' 'Why don't parents trust us to look after ourselves?' There were always questions on 'petting' in the form of 'How far can you go?' Attempts were made to draw the line between 'petting', 'heavy petting' and 'going the whole way'. (I do not know if the word 'petting' is still in use.) Rape was raised infrequently, and the response from girls was that the girl was to blame for leading the man on. There was general agreement that men were much less able than women to control their sexual impulses and allowance had to be made for this fact.

In older groups, engagement and marriage were talked about. I do not remember the question of divorce being raised. In discussion on money within marriage, the general view among girls was that the money the husband earned was his own and he should have control of it, otherwise 'you were treating a man like a child'. A very small minority thought that money should be managed jointly between husband and wife.

I have no way of judging what effect, if any, these discussions had on the young people who took part. They were always completely absorbed and time passed very quickly. They often thanked me politely and sometimes added, 'Don't you mind talking about these things, my Mum wouldn't like to.' The Abortion Law was passed in 1967, as well as the Sexual Offences (Amendment) Act. The Pill arrived with no warning of its possible dangers. Drugs were becoming available and 'bouncy pills' were handed out freely to those who were tense or depressed. Women's liberation was on the horizon and it looked as though there was free choice for all.

The story of Mary, perhaps, best illustrates the end of an era. It occurred between October 1966 and May 1967. Mary, a very intelligent and enthusiastic student, came up to a university, the first in her family to do so. She had a place in a hall of residence. After a few weeks she found she was pregnant and reported this to the Warden of the hall. She did not want to be in touch with the father of the baby. She had written to her family, who refused any kind of contact or support. The possibility of abortion was never mentioned either by Mary or anyone else. She was visited by the Chaplain, and after much anxious discussion by the staff, Mary was advised not to mix with the other students and to wait until the Chaplain found her a place in a Mother and Baby Home. From there she wrote me long letters describing not only the progress of her pregnancy, but also the rigid and oppressive atmosphere. She did not lose her sense of humour and on one occasion wrote a hilarious account of the obligatory visit to church on Sunday mornings of twelve women in various states of pregnancy trying to fit into the pews.

Mary had her baby in hospital and arranged for him to be given for adoption. Her mother visited her just before she left hospital, their first contact since Mary had written to her family about being pregnant. The baby was kept in a nursery and neither Mary nor her mother mentioned him. A nurse later reported to Mary that before her mother left she had asked to see the baby.

The student revolution of 1968 opened up the quest for yet new freedoms, with demands for greater control over university management and the subjects studied. I find it difficult to describe the impact of these demands on those of us who had accepted that our pastors and masters knew best. How, in any case, could you decide what you wanted to learn when you had not yet been introduced to what was available? At the same time women's liberation was becoming known in this country, proclaiming the fact, which I found even more extraordinary, that women were an oppressed class, both domestically and in the market-place. As the mother of daughters beginning their adult life, I found it very difficult to be a guide in a world which seemed so new and strange to me, as well as being confronted, often painfully, with looking at my own life.

I do not think it was entirely true to say that as parents we felt 'threatened', which was (and still is) popular parlance for anyone who did not want to give up an entrenched position. It was more that we felt guilty for finding it difficult to adjust to a changed landscape. It was not that we did not see the sense in some of the demands which were presented as self-evident truths, it was more that we did not know how to react without abandoning many of the beliefs we still thought were good. To put it another way, how could we find a meeting point between giving our children the benefit of our past experience, which we still thought valid and useful, and the different future they envisaged.

It is the case, however, that everyday life continues. Meals have to be prepared, whoever does it; children have to be cared for even if, ideally, their care is now shared. Adolescents need guidelines in sexual relationships in a world which has changed once again with fears about the Pill, questions about abortion, and the advent of Aids. In their turn our children will be confronted by many of the problems we faced. I wonder if they will find it easier to be open-minded because they have been more open and self-conscious about the world they are living in?

I had always hoped I would have a continuing relationship with my children when they grew up, although I think I accepted that this was, in a way, a matter of luck. It would depend on the kind of people they became and whether we still had things to share apart from the past. What I had not expected was that my children would educate me in any profound sense. I could not have expected that my daughters would introduce me to a new feminist world which would stand me on my head and cause me to question so many beliefs that I had taken so much for granted. I listened with interest to their views and those of their contemporaries. It took me some time to realise or to accept that this turnabout had something to do with me as well. I was already well on into middle age and it was difficult to see what I could do with this new view of women's place. As important, perhaps, how could I look back at my past without undervaluing or even negating the way in which I had spent my time? These are questions I still have to answer satisfactorily.

Notes
1. *The Care of Young Babies*, Dr John Gibbens, J & A Churchill Ltd., 1940.

AN INTERVIEW WITH
'Jane'

Unwomanly and
Unnatural – Some
Thoughts on the Pill

I got married in 1959, straight out of college – teachers' training college. I was just twenty-one. I was terribly in love with my husband, so I thought I ought to marry him. I think my parents were disappointed, actually, and anxious. My father was a doctor, an old fashioned sort of country doctor, and they wanted me to do something with my life. Just before the wedding I had a funny conversation with my mother – she was discreetly trying to find out if I was getting married because I was pregnant, and to tell me I didn't have to, that they would 'stand by me'. What was funny about it is that I was furious, outraged; how dare she suggest that Tom, my husband, was like that!

It was also funny because by the end of the honeymoon I *was* pregnant. It certainly wasn't planned. We were supposed to be using the cap, but honestly I think I was so innocent that I'm not sure I was even using it right. And I hated it. I found putting it in and out totally disgusting, and silly: you know, running to the bathroom the moment the mood struck and then fiddling about and then putting on a pretty nightie and running back to the bedroom, and Tom pretending he didn't know what I had been doing. I think he was pretty innocent too, I mean about contraception – his line, if we had ever discussed it, would have been that it was nothing to do with him.

Anyway, there I was pregnant, and it all seemed rather romantic and we were very happy and sweet and not really bogged down financially. And it was all right, I loved having the baby and that gave me enough to do, and we moved to a house. And then I was pregnant again. There were fifteen months between Sue and Caroline, which wasn't enough but it wasn't impossible either. By now I had somehow gleaned enough information to be using the thing all the time, and cream, though I still found it revolting, so it was simply contraceptive failure, and that made me angry. I was angry with Tom, but inside I really agreed with him that it was nothing to do with him, so I think I was angry with myself and angry with life. But I couldn't be angry with the girls, could I?

After Caroline was born I was anxious all the time and found it hard to speak to Tom about it, so it was those old routines about having headaches and being terribly tired, which may explain why it took me over a year to get pregnant again. Tom was angry, which is funny now but not then, and I was miserable. But somehow I persuaded myself that it was the last time and I would like a little boy, and everyone kept saying what a lovely family and Tom was doing well and I sort of came around to it. And then what happened was I had a late miscarriage. Nearly twenty weeks. It was horrid. I think it was the worst thing that has ever happened to me in all my life, actually. And then when I went to the doctor for the check-up afterwards he said something about waiting a little while before trying again, and quite suddenly – and I wasn't that sort of person – I burst into floods of tears, just cried and cried and said that I couldn't, I couldn't do it again, I just couldn't bear it and I hated the cap and it didn't work and Tom didn't understand and all those things. I think the doctor said something about 'baby blues' and grief and I just went on saying that I couldn't, I couldn't go through it again, I would rather be dead. And part of me was as surprised as he was and part of me knew that it was true.

And then he said there was this new thing called the Pill that you just took in the morning. I know this sounds odd but I hadn't even heard of it. I don't think he had ever prescribed it before himself. He was really sensible and nice about it too, admitted that he didn't know a lot about it and I should go and see someone in London and he would write a letter for me and so on.

It was completely wonderful. It changed my life. I don't mean overnight. I can't remember now how I felt at first. But soon, I felt in control, I felt free, if I had known then what we know now about it how dangerous and so on it is I don't think I would have cared. Before I'd been on it a year I had an affair; not because I was in love with the man, nor because I hated Tom – I think now I did it just because I could do it and get away with it. I felt so wonderfully clever. Women say now that the Pill was just a man's plot so that women would be more available, but they can't be serious. I mean whatever it was for wild and whacky students, for provincial married women like me it was wonderful. They would have to be women who can't remember what it was like before: worrying all the time and all that messing about. Sex belonged to me, not to Tom and to the children.

It wasn't just the Pill of course. But the Pill did something else too, it made sex news. There were other things that happened about then, the Christine Keeler business and the Lady Chatterley case; suddenly you could talk about sex at dinner parties, because it was in the newspapers. So then you could talk about it; ordinary, respectable, married women could sit round dinner tables and talk about it. It wasn't the Big Secret. But it was the Pill, I think, that made it possible for things to change, for women to find out about fun. I don't like it when people say it was a bad thing, I just think they don't know what they are talking about. I never really got involved in women's lib, but I do feel sympathetic to lots of those things; and I do think it was the Pill that made it possible. All the things that have happened for women since, that I see in my daughters, I think they wouldn't have happened without the Pill.

It did change things for me, not just in the bedroom. I

mean it meant I could understand why students, why unmarried women might want it too. And then why homosexuals would want to do that. It made me more liberal I think. It made me braver, just that knowing that you didn't have to be sure about a man, be sure that he would stand by you before you took any risks. Sex was not a big risk any more, and nor were men. I said how I had been angry when Tom seemed to feel that it wasn't his business. Well, I realised that it wasn't his business, it was mine, and I could manage it all on my own.

I didn't stay on the Pill very long, less than ten years. It just seemed to get too dangerous. But even after I changed I didn't lose that feeling that the Pill had given me. That I was allowed to have what I liked and did not have to be frightened of sex because it could trap me into things, I didn't have to be punished. I look at the girls now – Caroline is married and Sue isn't – and I think I just don't have to worry about them in the same way. I mean I do worry about them of course, but it's different. They don't know how lucky they are, and that's nice.

Marsha Rowe

Up from Down Under

If you look long enough into the abyss they say you only see yourself. I see, a long way away, a girl in a turquoise blue uniform hunched over her school desk. It is me at fifteen years old, in my fourth year at high school. It is Sydney,

Australia, 1960. The class room is a prefab with a verandah. My best friend left school the year before and I am deciding that the best way to ward off loneliness is to compliment someone at school every day. These images fade fast. The blue uniforms. The heat. The dappled shade of the eucalyptus.

It is Saturday night. She walks slowly over the grass between the Chinese lanterns in the trees and down some steps on to a patio. She wears a dress she sewed with her mother of white furnishing cotton patterned in red hibiscus. Her friend takes her hand, Come with me. And she leads her into the bathroom. They can hear the party music outside where the others are jiving, hand in hand, turning, twisting. Her friend squats, whips something neat, small and glistening out of her bag, peels off its cellophane wrapping, wings her arms round and under her thighs over the toilet. What's that? What are you doing?, the girl asks. Changing my Tampax, she answers.

The girl buys some tampons the next weekend. She squats on the tiled floor of the shower room. Two hours later she is still there. The soft folds of flesh between her legs are a barrier. She cannot find the hole. She knows the blood comes out but she is not sure where from and does not know the words for what she does not know, such as vagina or cervix or labia. She knows the word womb but cannot relate it to her body. She cannot take this word womb inside her and say it is there, in that place, in me. She moans softly and admits she has to give up this search. She says nothing about this to her mother. She and her mother never speak of such things.

The sun is so bright that even the shadows bounce with colour. She is seventeen, going through the tall, iron gates of the university on the first day of her first job. She wears a candy-striped dress, slingbacks, white cotton lace gloves and plastic bracelets to match the blues and greens of her dress. Her skills are shorthand at 110 words a minute and typing at 40 words a minute. Five days a week she fights to stay awake while the various heads of laboratories dictate letters at a very slow speed. And she types. She types and types. She copies columns of figures, the results of lab tests. These are legal documents and must be right in every respect. No corrections. A mistake means starting the page again. She becomes excellent on the tab bar.

Downstairs at lunchtimes her boyfriend waits to see her, a well-off young student whose father is soon to die. After he dies no one cleans the swimming-pool in the garden of his parents' house. He rings her at home one Saturday and tells her that President Kennedy has been shot.

At work two of the doctors, including the one woman doctor in the labs, die. There is a scandal and a mystery. Death by drowning or by pills, murder or suicide, by the river, or in the nearby bush. She does not understand the stories in the newspapers. No one at work seems to know what really happened.

At lunchtime and on some evenings she goes to lectures in English and Philosophy. Her father, ashamed at his own lack of education, will provide for his sons' but not for his daughters' further education. She is paying her fees herself. She takes her young English tutor to see Joseph Losey's *The Servant*. She smokes Alpine cigarettes.

The appearance of things. When she wants a pageboy hairstyle for her first dance she ventures into the local hairdresser's. She has dark, wavy hair. No. It is impossible to look like the girl in the American leaflet about menstruation once handed out at school, impossible to have that smooth blondeness, a pageboy, the ends turned under, swinging forward as the girl in the photo bends her head demurely. She buys *Glamour* magazine. She laps up the images like a cat. She reads about a New York hairdresser called Kenneth. She sees a picture of him with a dark-haired model whose hair is short as a boy's. She goes back to a hairdresser to try again. Then she discovers the virtues of sticky tape. She peels it off and her fringe is dried without curls.

She has a straight nose with broad nostrils, very dark eyes and the sort of lips and eyelids which make people ask her, Are you Malaysian? Are you Polynesian? Half Chinese? Japanese? No, she answers primly. The White Australia

155

policy still restricts immigration on the basis of colour. In each question she sees the shadow of her father, cringing, unable to laugh off the racist taunts at school, being called Dago Joe for his similar dark eyes, dark curling hair.

She is finding a way to negotiate appearances. She designs an Eartha Kitt dress and, though it is made of pink wool, it is sleeveless, with arm holes cut back to expose the point of her protruding collar bones. She gives up wishing she were rounded, smooth and blonde. She gives up her virginity as well. One night when she sees the harbour lights from her boyfriend's friend's flat white like stars she feels the sharp pain as he ruptures her hymen. Afterwards she looks at the dark red stars on the sheets and tells her boyfriend it is all over between them. She goes back to typing, writing essays on English and US literature, falling asleep on the ferry on the way home, wanting to be somewhere else, to be someone else.

She sees *Oz* magazine on the news-stand. She sees it again. She sees the issue with the cover photo which gets them into trouble with the law, the three young men whose backs are turned as if they are peeing into the wall fountain of the fancy new Sydney building. Pissing on the city fathers. She does not dare to buy the magazine. Then she buys it. She sees the ad. For a secretary for the magazine. At the interview she jokes, What are your pension arrangements? She goes to work at *Oz* magazine in an office which is half a room rented from an estate agent who keeps his files in old cabinets. There is a creaking lift and a lot of dust. Sometimes she takes the train across the Harbour Bridge into work. Leaving Wynyard Station she sees mothers in the park with their placards, Don't send our sons to Vietnam. She senses the new apprehension as young men are drafted by lottery. Two boys she knows are going. Their names came up on the lottery. One of them never comes back. Others are winning money on the lottery for the building of the Opera House. She watches the young men in the *Oz* office and meets other young women who dash in with them. On rickety old tables the magazine is put together, pictures cut out, headlines and bylines dreamed up, cartoons drawn. The laughter and jokes are hilarious.

Posters. One poster is of the singer PJB, his body oiled, glowing in black and white. After a Sunday newspaper campaigns against his appearance, *Oz* is promoting him. With two of the *Oz* young men she visits PJB in his hotel. The groupies are giggling as PJB fondles them on the couch and pushes a vibrator down between their skirts. She walks out on to the hotel balcony. She pretends she is not there at all. She has not the pride to leave. Back at the office she watches one of the cartoonists, GS, scratching with a black pen on white glossy paper. He scratches and scratches like a hen at the paper. Black marks. Making a picture. Of a man. It is an aborigine. A black man. GS draws more than one picture. He draws an aborigine hanging on the cross. They choose that picture for the *Oz* cover. The referendum is held. Aborigines gain voting rights for the first time. Aborigines are still shadows also.

She leaves home. She stays in a house in Paddington which belongs to one of her friends. This friend, T, is on holiday. In fact, it does not belong to her. T rents it. In the back bedroom a boy sleeps with his lover. Every morning she sees their two male bodies entwined on the bed. She is their alarm clock. She wakes them up, as they asked her to. One weekend they spend a day of wandering along the beach. She and the boy peer into rock pools, into the clear, pale green water. Back to the house. Dylan songs. The tracery of ironwork on the verandah. The frangipani tree. The heat. The boy and she are together for the first time, that afternoon. That their two bodies can join, can lace together in joy and mystery. His former boyfriend is furious. Writes mean letters: 'All she does is break milk bottles.'

She is clumsy then in the kitchen and does not do the washing up after the lover holds his elegant Sunday lunches when the table is seated with beautiful men. When her friend returns from holiday there is a party, at which she and her boyfriend's ex-lover fight and never speak again. The party is for the Rolling Stones who are touring. Another friend sulks because Jagger will not remember her from the previous visit and will have another groupie for the night. At the party the rhythm and blues band plays, PLJ, which has become their local band. After the holiday there are two new members of the band who had arrived via Darwin that summer from England, a singer and a rhythm guitarist.

There are four women friends, T and A and J and herself. Two of them have long straight blonde hair soft as water. One is later to receive striped mini-dresses made of cotton jersey, presents from her boyfriend who has gone to London. He writes that he lives in a building called The Pheasantry on the King's Road. She will soon fly to join him. She was one of the first to go. There. Overseas. Overseas means England or Greece. For the gay men it is Greece. And for the others it is London.

But not yet. In the meantime there is the band. Three of the friends become lovers with men in the band. They find a building where they can play every Saturday night. Make their own disco. An old stone corner house. There are some chairs, mattresses, bits of crockery. The music is louder and louder and louder. ML's rhythm guitar. The dancers swim in the dim light. The singer, later to be gaoled for dealing, is gaunt. His blue eyes crackle with lights on stage and go empty, pale and defensive off stage.

When the music first changed from rock to rhythm and blues, she danced faster and faster until she was dancing inside the beat, inside the rhythm, to her own rhythm. She sweated. Her dresses clung to her back. She did not hear the words and the music possessed her. She finds another way to dance. She dances outside the music. She shuffles, pigeon-toed, keeping her torso straight, her arms free. Her body separates into different parts. When the band becomes professional, tours, and their disco moves to a city basement with bouncers at the door, the flashing strobe lights cut all the dancers into parts.

Nova magazine appears on the news-stand. Colour. Full page colour photos. Colour bleeding to the edge of the paper. No frames. Closer and closer to the texture. The pores of a lemon. The scales of hair. As if the print of the photo can go beyond the microscopic surface of things and surrender some greater truth. To the eye of the consumer.

Fashion takes up the football shirt. The style of stripes changes from vertical to horizontal. One of her friends is to be married wearing a trouser suit of cotton in horizontal stripes. She sews the shirt to match the trousers for her friend, with French seams, a white piqué double shirt collar and cuffs. At the wedding party she smokes her first joint. She looks down at the pink ice-cream melting in the bowl on her lap. She puts the bowl down on the low table in front of her. She sees she has put the bowl upside down. She walks out to the garden, out into the sweet, papery scent of the azaleas.

She lives in a number of different houses. She finds she can be mean and possessive about money when she is the only breadwinner in a houseful of people. She leaves *Oz*. Is it possible to slide into another life, between the pages of another magazine, images of other lives? What is there? *Vogue Australia*. For the interview she wears a home-made, skimpy, silk flowered dress, her hair long. She is turned down. She is accepted in an import/export firm specialising in food parcels for missionaries in Malaysia. It is one of a series of temp jobs. A year later. She has sewn another dress. Smart, grey linen, white collar and cuffs. She has short hair again. She has left her boyfriend, she has moved back home. She gets the job. She rides in the ferry over the glistening harbour waves to work every day. She types advertising figures. Monthly running costs of a magazine. She finds out how the colour pages are printed. Examines colour separations. Visits the printer. Her boss at *Vogue* is kind, wants her to learn new skills. The *Vogue* glamour becomes familiar. The white cups of coffee from a percolator, the black and white tiles on the floor, the white desks, the shelves of Condé Nast magazines. More than she can read. She sews herself neat mini-dresses with box pleats like schoolgirl uniforms. Close up the gloss chips and cracks. Personal tragedies. The son of BM who sells advertising rides a motor scooter. No one bothers with helmets. He crashes, survives, his brain badly damaged.

She visits her friends. Three of them live with the band. The police knock at the door. She watches as someone stuffs pills under the sugar in a bowl. Someone else runs to the toilet out the back and coolly denies flushing away the joint. It is after work and she is wearing her *Vogue* office clothes. She has a cream leather Chanel satchel on a long chain handle. The chain rattles on her knees as she shakes in fright. She puts the bag on the floor. One of the policeman lifts the lid off a saucepan simmering on the stove. Cabbage. Is that all you've got to eat, he spits out. But they are gourmets. It is part of their meal. We despise the police. We are outside of the lives of the police.

She could stay at *Vogue*. What is the point. The lives of the rich. Nothing. She has never understood how anyone can leave Sydney, the blue, glistening harbour, the bays and inlets, the deep winter greens and grey of the water. One afternoon when she lives with friends again, with her friend T, who has a baby boy, she stands on the cliff over Bondi. The wind whips at her hair and salt spray stings her face. And she understands that she too has to leave.

She gets a job on a cruise ship returning to the Mediterranean for the European summer cruises. The company employ cashiers to prevent the barmen cheating. One barman shows her how they do it. He shakes the can of tomato juice upside down as if to pour out every last drop. He puts the can down and serves the drink. There is enough juice left in every can so that out of six cans he makes a new drink. Profit to the barman, one juice in six. The company clocks up hours of overtime. No one is paid a penny of that overtime. And at Southampton there is no time to argue about it. In the ship's hold she has a trunk-sized piece of musical equipment. For the band. The band and most of her friends are in London now. Some meet her at Southampton. They drive her up to London. She sees the pale, cloud-muffled sun, the pale English daffodils at the roadside. There are no bright contrasts of light and shade, nothing set into sharp relief, no clarity of outline. Except along the King's Road where she sees the girls wearing make-up bright as advertising on their pale English skins. Her Australian friends now wear velvets or drooping, faded print dresses and hide their ankles in boots.

She flees the all-embracing, permeating greyness even though the city makes her feel at home, makes her feel inconspicuous, less of an alien. She takes the train to Greece. On the train the sailors in the compartment complain that she smokes too much and protect her from a night-time intruder.

She finds a vacancy in a flat with two sisters from Nottingham who teach her how to chase away the cockroaches. They scream with laughter chasing the cockroaches. They also teach her how to find clients for English lessons. These pay the rent. She looks up an Australian friend who is married to a Greek. She meets many Greek people. She finds out that in the brightest of clear lights of Athens there is torture, the regime of the Colonels. She is told about the history as if it were yesterday. And today. The shutters are closed. The stories are often in whispers. The war. The civil war. The British betrayal. The resistance. The miles in bare feet searching for food during the war, the rafters burned for firewood. She turns up for one of her regular lessons. Her client, a journalist, is imprisoned. She drifts to an island with a Greek friend who paints pictures, sculpting wire across the figures in his paintings, red carnations for blood. With luck he'll get the paintings out to New York to make his protest. On the island, in the cool white room one afternoon, she is about to sleep. She is drifting up to the ceiling. She looks down at herself on the bed. She comes to with a shock. She understands she has to leave. Greece is not her place. She has to speak English again and to find a way to engage with the world now she has begun to wake up.

Back in London, a flat in Notting Hill Gate with some of the same band, and the same friends. The landlady wants them out. Strong men arrive at 3 a.m. and hoist their things on to the street. She ends up in Ealing. She has another job temping. She stands on Ealing Broadway station every morning. It snows and her feet ache with chilblains in the snow. How does anyone keep warm? She hallucinates police at the door when she is on acid. Snow blows in through the broken window and she retreats into a hot bath full of bubbles she makes with detergent. She types at her different jobs. Someone else finds another flat at Notting Hill. She goes there, again with T. and the baby, from before. She dances in pubs on Saturday nights when the band plays.

RN suggests she return to *Oz* and she agrees. In the flat she piles her old brightly coloured mini-dresses on the bed. She finds a pair of scissors. One by one she cuts the dresses into shreds. She buys some calf length old print dresses and a pair of Biba canvas boots. She looks the part. At the *Oz* office she sweeps the floor with a dustpan and brush. She types. She answers the phone. She arrives early.

At night the colours glow brightly again, velvets and silks like stained glass. At the Electric Cinema light shows accompany the music and strangers pass joints down the row. Women dance with grace, swaying like wheat, while men jump like grasshoppers and wag their bottoms like Jagger. The music is a tornado one minute and small as a bird the next. They smoke a lot of hash and develop a moral grading of dope, from soft to hard. Marijuana is sensual, self-enlightening and non-violent; acid is enlightening on a more powerful scale, and more of a risk – by going beyond your ego you found a higher self or you never came back; a heroin habit need not be self-destructive, but who could afford it, and since it cushioned the ego it was self-indulgent; cocaine promoted cynicism; speed, mandies, sleepers were for kicks. On acid she finds that the orgasm of sex pulsates forever until she is on a perfumed island of desire. But also frightening little orange fish zap out of nowhere into her glass of water and the supermarket fluorescent lights shoot blue arrows which dig into her skin and pierce her flesh. Appearances are misleading. Despite the drugs which take her through appearances and apparently out the other side, she discovers a way of brushing her hair so that it dries straight. She maintains the vanity of appearances. She maintains the independence of earning enough to live on and to pay the rent. It would not be cool to admit she is not having fun.

In this land of grey shadow it is enough to be Australian. The Australians protect each other from the British sneers, no culture, philistines. Passports, work visas, length of stay. They sort things out. They leave, come back, leave.

The summer of the Isle of Wight festival. She works the stencil machine in the *Oz/Frendz* tent where they publish a festival news-sheet every few hours. She types the stories which come in. From the Release tent, for anyone in trouble with the police, over drugs, having a bad trip. French anarchists try to pull down the fence. The organisers accede to the demand that the festival be free. The softness of girlfriends who do not work the stencil machine and wear mint and pistachio dresses of silk. She is not one of them. Afterwards she remembers the fields of mud and litter, mascara running down cheeks in the rain, Jimi Hendrix on stage and one of the school kids who had worked on the *Oz* school kids' issue running in weeping, 'It's the end. It's dying.'

The issue of *Oz* which was put together by school kids has a cartoon of Rupert Bear with an oversized prick fucking Honey Bunch K, the US girl-momma figure. It is puerile, rebellious and not pornographic. At the *Oz* trial she realises the importance of Rupert Bear in the British psyche. The judge peers at the cover, the blue and grey tinted photo of the tall, elegant, naked woman. He asks, What is she doing with that? Is that a tail between her legs? Is it a rat?

She is up night after night taking shorthand notes, typing, seeing witnesses, the evidence being prepared. Typing. Typing. The trial of the *Little Red School Book* will follow the *Oz* trial. The young demand to be respected, listened to. She wears cream satin trousers to the *Oz* trial which are too tight and uncomfortable. Appearances. *Oz* changes after the trial. It becomes a vehicle for selling records. Commercial. She and J, a gay man, argue fiercely with FD of *Oz* that the photo of a naked female figure straddling the US eagle is obscene. It has no redeeming aesthetic nor any political allegorical point. It is lewd, pornographic. Fine lines between appearances. She and J lose the argument. J returns after a gay liberation meeting. He is unusually serious, confused. The lesbian women want to separate and to have an autonomous movement.

The Female Eunuch is published. The launch party is crowded. The bass guitarist of the band has been talking about this book G was writing, working really hard on it, like every day. She does not read the book then but does go to G's house in Italy to recover from the *Oz* trial. The money she earned typing was stolen but L pays for her ticket. She is dependent on her friend L. In Italy she and L pluck chickens in the sun and listen to G's stories in the evening. G drives her moped south to Rome for a dinner party. She does not wear pants. During the dinner she looks down and sees her pubic hairs sticking out through the silk weave threads of her dress. G says to her, I need a secretary. Would you like the job? She thinks, type, type, type. No, she answers. She pines for her new boyfriend. She returns to Britain. They make love in an outhouse in a field in Ireland. She knows she is pregnant. Later she checks it out. She is right.

Ink newspaper is launched despite the deep weariness after the *Oz* trial, everyone shattered. But still this newspaper. One woman journalist works on the paper but otherwise women only service the production of the paper. And still the dope. She accepts mescaline one lunchtime from a friend just back from the States. It's real natural stuff, man, organic. High on mescaline she laughs and laughs at the *Ink* staff sitting round the office, seeing them as a company of little animal folk, brown bears, grey bears, mice, owls, moles. And after she returns from Italy she resigns. It is impossible to stay once the typesetters she had interviewed and organised had been fired while she had been away.

She finds another job, typing. Typing for DR from whom she borrows the abortion money. She has been living in various friends' flats and houses. She goes back to RN and L's basement flat in Notting Hill Gate. L shouts, Why don't either of you ever clean the flat. You expect me to do everything, you and R. Guiltily she cleans. R cleans and learns to cook. Men like R take to making curries. It is an art form. The sniffing and grinding and mixing of spices. They can cook without having to identify with their mothers.

With L and J she demonstrates outside the Albert Hall on the night of Miss World. Candles splutter. Banners. Glitter. J, her gay friend, wears a silver dress and purple eyeshadow. And only a few months before she had been with these two same friends to an Alternative Miss World. A satirical event, a happening, like Warhol. A party to be filmed for a painter J knew. Hockney. She had worn her Biba shorts and boots and walked along a low platform between flowers in the bright camera lights. Self consciously. And then and now. The night glittering. The banners. The Albert Hall protest. And inside. Inside her. Her womb. Her pregnancy. Her breasts swelling.

Soon afterwards she has the abortion. She is suicidal. Anguish and anger. She thinks she has simultaneously discovered and denied her womanhood in the abortion. Yet she cannot reduce womanhood to biology. She refuses any simple conjunction of mind and body. She cannot integrate the physical and the mental, and her ideas about these split further into separate spheres. She does not yet know how to forgo this simplistic duality. Appearances. If she goes on and on fast enough she will appear whole. Just as separate lines or dots of colour appear to join on a spinning top and to appear as one. Instead of giving birth to a baby she will give birth to a magazine for women. She and L have the first meeting of the women who work in the underground press. Out of these meetings comes *Spare Rib* magazine.

It was not until January 1987 that I saw images which took me back to the experience of the sixties. These were paintings by Anselm Kiefer, a German born in 1947, of my generation. They were exhibited in a gallery in Amsterdam. The paintings were very large. Some took up entire walls. They were paintings of war. Steel, rusting iron, grey seas, destroyers, barren ground, mausoleums and monuments. They were paintings of witness and remembrance and recalling, of the Second World War, of wars in the present and of wars possible in the future. They were War in the abstract. Death. Destruction. Their grey, gritty surfaces were the intimate images of my dreams and nightmares throughout the sixties. I saw then that I had been carrying lives not my own; that our generation had also lived out the youthful irresponsibility which our parents, who had grown up knowing only war, thrift and responsibility, had been denied; that the sixties was an experience also of the generation before us – their own thwarted youth and yearning for freedom from constraint and their unfulfilled desire to throw cares to the wind, a desire that fitted into a market, a generation with money to spend.

Our youthful communing across nationality, class, race,

dissolving our individuality into a tribal, familial group and our collective living out of pleasure had kept us also chained unconsciously to an unrecognised past of pain and death. It kept us from seeing through appearances. The sixties was one long Indian summer of shining brightness, long hair, short dresses, long legs. It was also an experience of metaphysical joy and utopian sharing. One long summer with its shadows which still stretch into the future, knowing the waste land is not behind us.

AN INTERVIEW WITH
Julie Christie

Everybody's Darling

Five years ago I might not have been interested in talking about the sixties, but now I have a new theory. The sixties have a terrible relevance now, today, with this renewed onslaught of consumerism. Looking back, it seems that one of the good things about the sixties was that a generation of people grew up who were sick to death with the values, the same values of consumerism, that are turning us into mad people nowadays, just pouring into their heads this 'Buy! Buy! Buy!' which is so similar to the fifties. With new wealth, new markets had to found, and the advertisers were finding these different markets. The Youth Market was suddenly found. 'Gosh! Youth has a little bit more money. Let's make them spend. Working-class people have a little bit more money. Let's make them spend.' So there was all this advertising and new markets being created, and that's happening now too; all these different sub-classes that are being invented and targeted – women more now, and very young children.

One of the things that was good about the sixties was the reaction to all this. Culture had an element of austerity about it: how little you could do with, rather than how much you could get, became in itself a kind of status. And with that there was a real consciousness about the state of the world – and the powers of the establishment really had to stamp that out; because the culture of the sixties was fundamentally anti-capitalist, anti-multinationalist; it was dangerous in that sense. And with that real internationalism came the beginning of an ecological awareness which was a wonderful thing, and has never quite died, never been killed. Ecology, the simple idea that we're responsible for the earth as the earth will be responsible for us, and that everything affects everything else, really does stem from the sixties; from the hard work of people then suddenly realising that the world and ourselves were not disconnected and then trying to do something about it. It was a very responsible era in a way. There were as many responsible people as there were jumping out of it – drug-crazed people – but they're forgotten. Truly an awful lot of people were really willing to take on responsibility, not be apathetic. Whether they were stoned or not really didn't matter. Sometimes being stoned helped you to perceive things that were hidden from you by all the advertising; perhaps getting stoned was the only way to overthrow this sort of mind-fucking that had been going on, this brainwashing. Although there were a lot of casualties, it wasn't such a bad thing – trying to get on to another plane.

And all this was important to me. I didn't do very drastic drugs, at least I didn't do them very much. I'm too much of a coward. But I certainly was affected by the whole need to understand why we're here, what life is about. I was interested in the spiritual level of these sorts of issues. I didn't get into any spiritual cults, but I was very much part of that longing for some way of making sense of the whole mess. I started to read Buddhist books, which were not at all feminist – I wasn't looking for that then – but did open my eyes to the spiritual issue; and I believe that the ecology movement came out of that spirituality.

Certainly, although I wasn't very brave, one thing that was very strong to me was this consciousness that I must push through my self-imposed barriers. I didn't want to write in red on black or anything, like the people at *IT* were doing for instance: although I read it and enjoyed it because there were things in it that I could see were mind liberating, but I could never quite get over my annoyance at all those ink blobs and stuff. But it was breaking down a barrier. It was breaking down a code, the received code of how print is and how it should be. That's just an example. They were important experiments. For me it wasn't that barrier necessarily, but all sorts of other barriers, all the repressions and limitations that everybody has, and which in other terms are too easily accepted as 'natural' and I, along with so many other people, felt a constant need to try and push through so many things that were getting in my way, mainly because of fear.

On the other hand there was something I found very oppressive about that time: the peer pressure – the whole business of being as freaky as possible and if you weren't you were labelled 'straight' or 'square'. There was definitely status within that apparently no-status, 'classless' society. There was enormous status and it hung on how much drugs you took or how you dressed or just how freaky you were. I know I always felt I was on the outside looking in. I think the majority of people did. I was always on the fringes of people who I perceived as really being in the epicentre of the vortex. I felt like a country bumpkin who had for some reason found herself in this elevated society and had no idea how to handle it. But although it was a pressure it was not entirely a bad pressure, because it was to do with love, whatever it means. Love was seen as it is, although it's unfashionable now it is still one of the, perhaps the, most joyful feelings. Love of everybody – there were rare moments when you actually had the feeling that you were part of the human race and that we are all much of a muchness. I think that because some people had touched it in their drugged states, we were all trying to get there, get into that feeling permanently: and it is not a bad feeling.

I'm terribly grateful that it happened, and that I was around, because those values became the basis of how I still try to operate now. Although we were struggling against the status quo, we did establish a new status quo. If it hadn't become so easy to . . . perhaps if it hadn't become the fashion to incorporate those very high ideals, then probably I wouldn't have got in touch with that in myself at all, or anyway not until much later.

But having said that I must also say something else; something about the confusion about women's roles in the sixties. That, at least, has developed, while most things have regressed: women's standing, if not economically, not in state consciousness, at least in their own heads things have actually got better. Because in the sixties there was an awful lot of sex objectivism. In films, for example, women were there to be disliked by the heroes over and over and over again. They were treated so badly – I mean in *Room at the Top* and *Saturday Night and Sunday Morning* and almost all of the rest: they were all about boys who wanted to be free and wanted to screw lots of women, and they always had this person who they were expected to be faithful to, and that person was a nag and a whiner and a restriction on them. *Poor Cow* was a conspicuous exception – so much kinder, and more understanding, but Ken Loach has always been very progressive. I often wondered what it was that *Darling* offered that was new, because it must have offered something. I didn't see it then but now I realise that there weren't many images of men-free women at all, of a woman who would actually go out and pursue her own goal. That was *Darling*; whether she was condemned for it or not (and she was, in the end, wasn't she) – she was, extraordinary though it seems now, twenty years later, a brand new idea, in terms of film, of the media. Here was a woman who didn't want to get married, didn't want to have children like those other kitchen-sink heroines; no, Darling wanted to have *everything*. Of course at the time, this was seen as greedy promiscuity and she had to be punished for it. But there was an element of possibility for women, of a new way of living, which is why the film was such a success.

It was no fun for me that film, because I was working so hard. I went through it in a bad mood, just on the edge of tears all the time. And it was complicated. For example at the same time as I was making it I had broken through my fears of nudity. I was quite happy to take my clothes off on beaches. I did reach a level of a certain non-self-consciousness: a terrific achievement for me. It took a real struggle, a lot of effort. But in the film nudity was a horrible thing to do and I hated it. I think because I've always been aware that nudity on the screen, women's nudity at least, is always in some way exploitative, given the prurience that it always encourages in the viewer. Though as a matter of fact that prurient gig-gliness that goes with Page 3 now is actually worse. Back then of course you couldn't have had Page 3 girls. They would have been in *IT* or *Oz*, wouldn't they – trying to break through into 'free sexuality'.

Obviously a lot of what was going on wasn't thought out, it was all an experiment. But an important experiment. Certainly it was wonderful being part of it. I was in America in 1968, and everything seemed white-hot, there then. I was making *Petulia* in San Francisco, where everything was going on. There was Golden Gate Park where all the political demonstrations and the love-ins were. There was my own extremely hard work. There was – above all there was – that powerful sense of something new happening, and I was there. I will never forget the feel of it. The thing that stays most in my head though is the music. It was free – you didn't have to be a certain way, or freaky enough, or anything, for the music to have its effect on you. The Doors, Jimi Hendrix, Janis Joplin: the music was potent – it excited me and still somehow personifies the time, of excitement and break-through and danger.

YEARNING

'I'm on the dark side of the door'

Sheila MacLeod

A Fairy Story
....

Once upon a time in the magical year of 1963 when everything suddenly seemed possible, two Oxford graduates set up

home together in a flat near Primrose Hill. He wanted to be a rock star, she a writer. Both were brimming with ambition, innocent, narcissistic, in love. Both, above all, were young. And to be young in those days meant to be idealistic, enthusiastic and full of optimism about a future which was to be so dazzlingly, liberatingly different from the hidebound parental past.

Everything seemed to be changing: not as before on the margins of their lives where war, famine, coups or general elections could all be monitored from the corner of the eye, but right there in the intimate arena of their everyday lives. There was something in the air, something heady, an irresistible force meeting what had once been an immovable object and was known as the Establishment. Something was blowing in the wind, something each of my protagonists had first felt on the road from Aldermaston to Trafalgar Square. It was an almost holy feeling of solidarity with their ordinary fellow-creatures and a concomitant scorn and loathing for the powerful who could contemplate the destruction of the planet with insouciance. It was an angry but as yet good-humoured feeling of being right. And good. And bound to succeed.

Both my protagonists saw themselves as subversive. She was the more political of the two, had been arrested several times for civil disobedience, spent nights in police cells and told the magistrate the following morning, 'I'll do it again.' As a student she had written short stories which (she learned later) had made people feel uneasy. This had not been her intention. She had simply written frankly about sex, pain, uncertainty, her own feelings, in a time when it was fashionable to be clever rather than honest. She had intended to impress rather than to confound.

His passion was the Blues, the raunchy, earthy music of Black America from the Southern plantations to the ghettos of Chicago or Detroit. It represented everything his parents hated, as the glitter of show business mocked and minimised the solidity of their conventional lives. He saw himself as dangerous, but his aim was to *épater la bourgeoisie* (of which he was a member) rather than to turn the world upside down. As a student he had sung with a band and, being a good-looking fellow as well as a showman, had become something of a hero. The time was opportune for heroes of his sort.

Early in 1963 he auditioned as singer with one of the Blues-based groups which had appeared as if from nowhere in the wake of the Beatles' success. When he got the job and a salary of £15 per week, he was jubilant. At the same time she learned that her short stories were to be published in an anthology designed to introduce promising new writers to an adventurous reading public. She too was jubilant. What a charmed couple they were! Then a prestigious literary weekly offered her a job. But she was already pregnant and she turned it down.

She had always wanted children and was glad to be pregnant. Jobs could wait and, besides, he would soon be earning enough to support all three of them. The group was an instant success, their first single going straight to number one in the charts. It was taken up as the signature tune for an exciting new TV programme based on pop music and fashion and which soon became enormously popular. From then on she scarcely saw her husband who was always either away on tour or, when at home, working by night and sleeping by day. As far as his public was concerned, he was no one's husband, but eminently eligible, eminently available, and he, like the other members of the group, denied that he was married.

From now on I shan't attempt to chart his progress except as and when it impinges on hers. The lives of rock stars are well documented elsewhere and, alas, all too predictable.

For the most part she was content and when she was not, attributed her malaise to her pregnancy. Sometimes, isolated as she now was from friends and acquaintances by his sudden fame, she felt lonely, but the thought of the coming baby comforted her. Sometimes, when she sat with her knitting in front of the television, she felt frightened, as when she watched pictures of the 'forgotten war' taking place in a country she had hardly heard of: Vietnam. Her child kicking inside her, she flinched from the easy, haphazard slaughter which seemed to desecrate the laborious business of birth.

Her son was born in hospital, an easy birth, but he cried a lot and hardly slept. Her mother told her that she had been just the same, and she warmed protectively towards her demanding child. She also felt very close to her mother at this time. But for the most part she coped alone, snatching sleep day and night whenever the baby slept. One evening when they were both nodding off in front of the television there came a portentous announcement: President Kennedy had been shot. She was surprised at how personally she took the news, strangely aware of being present at an historic occasion, another moment of change.

Her life was taken up with her son. It was a slow, persistent business, built on details, beset by anxieties and illuminated by all sorts of unexpected delights. Her husband's life was the world of the group, the speedy, hyped-up world of sex and drugs and rock and roll where the race is to the fittest and the weak or unsuccessful are derided and exploited. She had imagined, in a schoolgirlish way, that it would be glamorous. And so it was. But she was no longer a schoolgirl. She had not imagined that that world could be so silly. Or so cruel. She had begun to despise it. And, inevitably, the marriage fell apart.

But not for long. When they discovered that she was pregnant again, they decided to give it another chance. It was only after the birth of their second son that they became really affluent and money helped to heal the breach. They bought a house in a fashionable area of London, enagaged a nanny, au pair, cleaning-woman, chauffeur. They made new friends who were equally rich and famous and successful. After an unfortunate but minor setback, the good times had begun to roll again. Or so they persuaded themselves.

His fame was then at its height and such as it is almost impossible to believe in these more sober times. He couldn't walk down the street or visit a supermarket, cinema or park without being recognised and, as often as not, mobbed. Girls waited outside the house or telephoned at unsocial hours. His hair was pulled, his clothes ripped. Once, in Manchester, it happened to her too and she was scratched and bruised.

When she escaped to join him in the waiting limo, the mob gathered round and rocked the car back and forth so that it was in danger of turning over. It was terrifying.

When he wrote a piece for a Sunday colour magazine about two (female) fans following him into the Gents, someone at the BBC picked up on it and asked him to turn it into a television play. He asked her help and, because he was never in one place for long enough to write anything, she wrote it all herself, sitting up in bed after the birth of her second son. The play, which went out under their joint names, was shown later that year. It was the first thing she had written since the birth of her children.

She would probably be ashamed of it now. It was no friend to her own sex, who were portrayed as adulatory masochists. But then such had recently been her most potent experience of them. It shamed her on behalf of all femininity to see how easily they allowed themselves to be exploited, how ready they were to offer and abase themselves. Sometimes she felt sorry for the young girls who wept their ecstasy or their disappointment in the face of their idols, but she had no time for the older women in their thirties or forties who were sly and catty and asked prurient questions. There is nothing like being married to a famous, and therefore desirable, man for showing you women at their very worst.

Needless to say, she was no feminist then in the mid-sixties, but sometimes she found herself overcome by anger at the way the men in the group talked about the women in the adoring audiences. Mainly they were seen in terms of their appearance or of the promise of sexual fulfilment. Those who didn't measure up (and most didn't) were verbally despatched in a series of scathing obscenities. It was taken for granted that it was men who performed and women or girls who admired and worshipped. The males had become the desired objects, the females the pursuers, but although the men were now the quarry they managed to retain their power by relying on the solidarity of the pack. They strutted and swaggered like so many cockerels. When she told them so, they took it as a compliment.

At the same time, and perhaps by way of appeasement, the

rock wife herself had become a considerable asset. Whereas in the early sixties the stars had been enjoined to deny their marriages, by the end of the decade a suitable wife had become as much a symbol of conspicuous success as a suitable house or car. Suitable meant not only good-looking but right-looking: stylish and expensive. It meant public appearances at home and abroad as the happy, smiling, ever-supportive partner. It wasn't much of a role, she soon discovered, despite the perks. Once, at the Cannes Film Festival when she was walking along a red carpet with her husband, she was showered with bouquets by a cheering crowd who wanted to touch or kiss her. It was a moment of maximum unreality: bizarre, alienating.

Fame like that does things to you. It can't but. What it did to him I'll leave to your imagination. What it did to her was no less devastating.

She tried hard to reconcile the roles of good wife and good mother, which were often at odds, and in the process she somehow lost sight of herself. What she wanted to do (write fiction) meant slow thoughtful work in her own space and time. But the world he lived in was frenetic and constantly changing, full of new enthusiasms which soon fizzled out and new projects which rarely came to fruition. It was unconstructed, unconsidered and there was no follow-through. Eventually it overwhelmed her need to make sense of it and her own part in it.

First, like any Victorian neurasthenic whose sense of effectiveness had been thwarted, she took refuge in sensitivity and fatigue. One of her sons complained at school that his mother was always ill. Later she became anorexic, as she had been before in her teens. Her GP diagnosed endogenous depression and prescribed anti-depressives which she dutifully swallowed three times a day for the next seven years. She became withdrawn, almost affectless, more isolated than ever. No one seemed to notice. After all, in her skinny size 8 mini-skirts, she still looked the part of the star's wife. And that was what counted.

Come on, I can hear you say, why on earth should we feel any sympathy for this poor little rich woman who hadn't the wit to recognise the roots of her own unhappiness? Good question. It was one she often asked herself. What reason, what right had she, who was the envy of so many, to be unhappy? She had been transformed into the princess in the fairy story. Isn't that what every little girl wants? But the irony of it all was that this little girl had never wanted any such thing.

Because she chose withdrawal rather than escape, you may well conclude that there were certain advantages to be gained from her apparent captivity. She thought so too and constantly enumerated them, as if to reassure herself. She loved her husband and children and was determined to make a success of the marriage against all the odds. They all needed her. She had status, security and an abundance of reflected glory. She could write (she wrote five novels in nine years) without having to worry about money or finding a job in the world outside show business, where her marriage would inevitably become an object of perpetual curiosity. She had made a bargain of sorts, and in theory it all worked very well.

In New York in 1970 she read Germaine Greer's *The Female Enuch*, which had a curiously familiar ring to it. It seemed to her like an abridged and popularised version of a book she had read ten years previously and very much admired: Simone de Beauvoir's *The Second Sex*. And she wondered at the gulf between theory (her intellectual endorsement of de Beauvoir's thesis) and practice (her own adoption of the traditional female role) in the intervening years. What had happened? Because it seemed as though something had happened to her rather than as though she had made her own decisions, except by default.

She was not alone. Now there was something else in the air, something of which Greer's book was only a symptom. It was an idea whose time had come and which became known as the women's movement. Its time had come because the sixties were over and eyes which had been clouded with 'peace and love' or psychotropic drugs were now wearily cold and clear.

The peace movement, which had never granted equal status to women, had culminated in several shows of violence, thus defeating itself. Love had been largely a matter of sex: as much sex as you could get with as many people as possible. Now it seemed no more than a greedy male fantasy of omnipotence. And the drugs which had promised ecstasy or oblivion had proved treacherous. Now the sixties looked very much like a male invention based in power, promiscuity and self-abuse.

The summary may sound harsh, but it was how she felt at the time. When she saw herself as a mini-skirted dolly bird she wondered how she could have been deceived into imagining that the fashions of the sixties spelled liberation for women. It now seemed that their purpose was to imprison women more securely as objects of male attention, male ribaldry, male lust. Whereas she had once been well disposed towards the so-called sexual revolution in that it substituted openness for hypocrisy, she now asked herself, revolution for whom? And she answered herself, for men, who could thereby indulge their preferences for irresponsibility and lack of emotional commitment. She had felt such things before, but dimly and helplessly, as a child resents the ways of the adult world, and she had been unable to articulate them.

It seemed to her later that a more optimistic view was possible, that the false liberation of the sixties had paved the way for the subsequent struggle towards a true definition of what it meant to be female and at least relatively free. To be aware of one sort of change could lead to an awareness of the necessity for other sorts. The men may have had it all their own way but, in doing so while preaching freedom, had brought their own preconceptions into question. Women who had maintained a traditionally subservient role in the proceedings began to realise sooner or later that they were still on the outside looking in at a world of unrestrainedly gratified desires and that nothing much had changed for them, whereas women who had tried to ape men's behaviour had discovered sooner or later through bitter and self-destructive experience that the world of male fantasy fulfilled did nothing to add to the sum of their own happiness. Maybe, after all, the sixties had been necessary.

Hers may not be a typical story, but it is by no means a unique one. Rather, it is an exaggerated version of what happened to many other women at the time. And, if it doesn't have the happy ending demanded by a fairy story, neither does it end in tragedy or despair. In fact, there is no ending. What she lived through in the sixties is still a part of her, much as she would sometimes like to deny it, and she can't write off the whole decade as a mistake, although she admits that mistakes were made by herself and by others. It is not mistakes as such which are reprehensible but the inability to learn from them. She still sees the sixties as a period of unmanageable turmoil, but also now as one of transition. They were going somewhere, namely here. And she is what she is today because she was what she was then.

AN INTERVIEW WITH
Gina Adamou

My Nose Pressed against
···
the Window
···················

I was born in Nicosia. My background was from a poor
working-class family, and I had a couple of aunts who were
married to English servicemen, and we had connections
through them, you know. So when one of my aunts came to
England it encouraged my parents to come over here. They
had, in fact, five daughters in Cyprus which meant that my
father had to be home, because you have to build the house or

buy a house for your daughter before she marries. No sons, no. Only five daughters. I'm the oldest of the girls. My parents came in early 1960, a few months earlier, to try to find a job and everything, and then they sent for us and so forth. So my grandmother came over here to deliver five kids. I was fifteen. I was born in 1945, so I was the oldest.

My first impression of London was love. I loved it. You know, I couldn't get over all the Christmas trees. The sight of these was like magic to me. I was much younger than my years, because we were very strictly brought up and not allowed to do anything, you know.

My father had two jobs, believe it or not. He used to be a carpenter during the day. He used to teach – he had a dance school. He used to teach dancing to young men in the evenings.

My mother was a dressmaker. Well, she used to make shirts, dresses, everything. She was good at her job. She used to work out. My grandmother brought us up. My grandmother who was always at home looking after us. My parents have both worked always in Cyprus and in England.

I should have gone to school in England, because I was still under age. I should have gone something like nine months or six months or whatever the time was. But they decided not to send me. In fact, they didn't even put my name down, which they should have done by the law, because they thought I was needed, because my grandmother was quite sick, at home. I had a younger sister of about four, very young, and I was the one to look after her.

The family kept me a whole year at home. I was very upset at the time, because they were expecting a lot of me. I was the one who had to look after my grandmother, my youngest sister, try to make some kind of a meal for my other sisters and parents coming home. In fact, I took the role of the householder if you know what I mean. They kept me home a whole year, but I must say this, that they must have felt guilty, because they had a teacher friend and they asked him to come and give me private English lessons at home.

I wanted to go to higher education, but being from my kind of background – my family didn't believe in girls going to higher education. In fact, I was very good at school. I used to write poems, stories. My parents thought education is for boys and not for girls. It is wasted on the girls. You know? They marry and so and so.

So the next best thing I would like to do is hairdressing. So they found somewhere to send me to learn hairdressing. I used to work in the shop during the day some time. Then I decided that I wanted a proper education, a diploma, so I said that I wanted to go to evening school. So I joined an evening school, and I qualified as a hairdresser – with my diploma and all.

But my parents were – what can I say? They were very strict. I wanted to have friends and go out and do all the things. They were against it. I wasn't allowed to do anything. When I came home, my father used to time us, you see. If you missed the bus, you know, and you were twenty minutes late, you have a lecture or they were suspicious: 'What have you been up to?' or things like that. They were really very strict. At the time I couldn't understand why, but now as I'm older I do understand it, because my parents were really young parents. They married very young. My father was very young. They lived in Cyprus which was very, very different. You didn't see couples cuddle and kiss in the street. So they come over here. All the people used to say things like, 'Look after the girls,' and 'This place is bad' and 'There's no morals'. Seeing young people kissing they didn't see that's what it was, just innocent affection between a couple. They thought, 'Oh, it was a bad place. Better look after the girls.' So it really was like a prison, you know. Everything at home on weekends. It was really – I wasn't happy at home. I wasn't allowed to have girlfriends at my home. No, no.

If we wanted to go to the cinema one of the parents – either my dad or my grandmother or somebody – had to come with us, you know, to escort us. We weren't allowed to go on our own. We used to be allowed to go for a walk in Chapel Market, but once me and my third sister we went there for a walk and somebody sort of commented. She went back and told my father, 'Oh, you know, there was a young man and he said this and that.' That was it. I was never allowed to go for a walk again. It was as if it was my fault if a young man complimented me.

My parents always had – it's funny now that I think of it, because they always had friends, they always liked to socialise themselves, but when it came to us they had different – you know what I mean? They had one rule for them and one for us sort of thing. I think they were really frightened, and it was their way of trying to protect us. Now I see this, but at the time I couldn't understand it at all. They were very, very strict, and our people used to arrange marriages for their girls and boys. They still do, a lot of them. That's what they tried to do for me. Again I refused, refused long . . . at that time I was even thinking of leaving home, but, of course, it wasn't easy. You know, it's not like now. I didn't know how to go anywhere.

So when my husband eventually came to ask for me or something, because they sort of arranged – the parents and the relatives arranged – for the young couple to see each other. I mean, they had to force me to go and see him, have a look at him anyway. I would rush off to the kitchen as soon as I could. After a while my dad followed me. He said, 'Why do you go there? A man is to call.' He said, 'You will like him.' And I remember that I kept thinking, 'Well, what do I know of him? I mean, I don't know the young man. Am I supposed to say, "Yes, I like him" or "No, I don't like him", because I don't know him.' That was my thoughts. He kept pressurising me on this. He kept saying things like, 'Well, put it this way, would you be ashamed to walk with him down the road for instance? Now just look at him.' 'No, why should I be ashamed to walk down the road? Why should I be ashamed to walk with *anybody* down the road?' I couldn't understand his reason. I'd stay in the kitchen and then people . . .

I was seventeen-and-a-half. He would come over to me and sort of say, 'Oh walk down'. Then I said yes I'd go down, and before I knew what had hit me I was engaged. I just couldn't believe it. I was shocked.

I knew that our people got married this way. I knew that similar girls did. I knew that the rest of the society didn't. Oh, yes. I was aware of that. But what choice do you have? My perception was within my head. I would say, 'No, no, no,' and then I started thinking perhaps it is one way of getting out, and I did think because I knew from other girls that I've seen once they're engaged they are treated completely different. One minute you are a child and you're not allowed to go from here to there. The next minute, because they put the engagement ring on your finger, you're an adult and you're allowed to do anything you want. So I thought perhaps this is the right idea. That it will give me freedom. It means I could go out and do this and that. And so that's what I did. I said, 'I'll marry him.'

As it turned out, I'm quite happy with my husband, who's a good man. But the real iffy thing of it is it's a gamble. I mean, it's like you throw a penny in there. It could come right or wrong. Completely a gamble. And I've got four sisters. They're all married in that way, and half of them are divorced now. They were all either married or engaged by the time they were eighteen. Some of them were younger. I mean, they didn't even give us a chance to grow up. I think they were scared, that we would get English, you know what I mean, and start having our own ideas. They wouldn't allow us.

I don't think I had a young life, as my own children have now, you know? I sort of left from my father and my mother and got engaged and married within six months. A year later I had my first baby. So I didn't really have much of a young carefree life like young people do. I remember I used to like Elvis Presley and I liked the Beatles. I mean, I couldn't do these things with my father, and then I couldn't do them with my husband.

I remember there used to be a club in Finsbury Park, and the Beatles used to play, just up the road, you know. I would have loved to go and see them, but he refused to go. He fought. He had old ideas. He used to call them 'hairy so-and-sos' – the Beatles which for me was exciting. I loved their music, and I wanted to go to the club, go in. I mean, I was only an eighteen-year-old, for God's sake. You know, I wanted to do the things the other eighteen-year-olds do. Another time I had a beehive. I used to wear my hair in a beehive. I used to get problems from my father and my mother and later from my husband. I mean, I used to get it from all sides. And I still used to do it. When it comes to fashion I still carried on, but my life was comments, comments all the time, if you like.

You know what I mean? I wanted to be one of them, you know, like other young people, but did I have a chance with my husband? No. It seems like you leave one man that says no to you and you find another one who says no. Within four years I had three children.

And then there was the racism also. In fact there were a couple of jobs – one especially sticks in my mind. One manageress really wanted to take me on. She liked me and everything, but she did say to me, 'I have to speak with my girls and see how they feel.' A little later the lady came back to apologise that the girls didn't want any Greek girl working there. I think it was the first experience for me of racism. I couldn't understand it. I mean, I was the same as them. I couldn't understand why. I mean, I spoke English, there was no reason. It upset me a great deal. I think it must have been the first time it was directed at me. I didn't get the job, because the girls didn't want a Greek girl.

After I was married there was a very sad time. We were very poor. We couldn't have, for example, a record-player. At home my parents did. As I said, my dad was involved in teaching dances, so we were very musical. We always had one at home. When I was at home, I used to save my pennies to buy these records – Elvis Presley and the Beatles records. But after when I was married, no. I left all my records at home. In fact, we couldn't afford to have a radio, anything. Not even a radio. It was a very, very lonely time, that time, because my husband used to work nights. I sat in my room with nothing to do. I tidied up the one room. I'd just sit in and read a book. Absolutely nothing. So after a while I got into a habit of finishing work and then going home to my mother, because I couldn't face going to that one room on my own. In fact, I was very unhappy, because I didn't even have my husband's companionship, if you know what I mean.

I still was servile. My husband's cousin who was a friend to me after we were married, he realised – he asked me what had gone wrong, and I told him. I said to him, 'He works all night and I won't go and sit in my room, so I go home to my parents every night just like I wasn't married.' I think he talked to my husband, because after that he started looking for a job in the daytime. And he found a job in a pastry shop. A few years later my dad started teaching him the job of carpentry and that's what he's doing until now. He was very loyal.

I think I still grudge my father. I still grudge the fact that with my children ... and I suppose it's envy. In fact, I'm bitter about it. It upsets me. It upsets me, because I didn't have a young life. If I had my own life I would have chosen – if I had a say I would have a different life altogether. I would have first of all gone to higher education, maybe a different work. Certainly I wouldn't have married until I was thirty. I'm afraid I didn't have much of a say in it, because, as I say, they brought us up so strictly. To think that under the circumstances I did have these thoughts in my head. I must have been already a very liberated woman. I am a liberated woman now – since. But, I mean, to think this way again under those circumstances must have been quite something. Last year he was here, my dad. He was trying to persuade me that I shouldn't let Christine – my daughter, Christine, is at the polytechnic. She's doing English and philosophy. He was trying to persuade me to give her a husband, not all this education. 'What does she want with all this higher education?' It upsets me.

Put it this way, I'm very much on my own. I'm sure there are women like me – but not very many. In all the Cypriot women I meet in my job here, I think I could really honestly say I met two or three. I mean, my own sisters – they think I'm too English. Even my husband says that I may look Greek, sound Greek, but I'm English. I don't think that at all. It's not English in my head. It's just being myself, being a woman, being an individual, having my own ideas, being the person that you are. Nothing to do with being English or Greek.

But yes, I'm very much me – not many like me, because unfortunately Cypriot men – they are bullies. They are bullies as fathers and then they are bullies as husbands. The women don't often – are not often allowed to find themselves, to find their own individual personality, whatever you want to call it. It's sort of – how can I put it – pressed out. Oppressed. I'm glad to see my girls haven't been like that. I would hate if they were that kind of pushovers.

I am a political person. I don't know my reasons. I am a political person, a very political person. I belong to the Labour Party because they represent something which I can understand, because I feel so angry with injustice. The unemployed, what is happening to a certain section of our society. Not that the Labour Party is perfect, but I believe it has some idea of the way I'm thinking, because I'm a very social-minded person. I'm one of the persons who likes to go around and make society better for all the people.

One of the things I want to do in this area is to encourage women to come out of their homes, encourage women to get involved. So I've been arguing for a local community centre in this area. There's a lot of house-bound women in this area. We must encourage them all to come and encourage them to have some sort of social life, because they're all home working. Their husbands go out. Sometimes they've got kids and sometimes not. They don't speak English. Yes, still. My neighbours still haven't learned. They became homeworkers when their kids were home. Twenty years later they still have the same job. Their kids, sometimes they are home, sometimes they are not. But they still do the same job. They're isolated. I mean, they come to me. If they want to go out to a job, it's a hundred thousand times more difficult. Even at the doctor's, even for the most personal things, I have to stand there, because they can't understand the language. These people have been twenty, twenty-five, thirty years in England. You know what I mean? They need in this area their community centre, somewhere to go, whether it is to have a cup of coffee, have some English lessons, do their own thing. That would encourage them to start thinking for themselves, start doing things for themselves. They must. I'm very, very anxious that we help to do that. From my own experience I don't know how but I feel very, very strongly. I'm so bitter about some of the lives Cypriot women live.

Yasmin Alibhai

Living By Proxy

I saw the sixties (proper) for the first time when Nadya
walked into the school party shimmering in a noisy silver

paper foil dress and hair which reached down three inches below the hemline, much of which she was air-propelling by the deft movement of her head from side to side with extraordinary viciousness. She was also showing a terrifying amount of leg. She cut through the crowd which was paralysed with horrific admiration and put on a Joan Baez tape, belting out some protest song. That too was a first.

This was Uganda soon after Independence; a time when all our social and political certainties as exile Asians were being dismantled. Much was beginning to happen. But for me, that day, fifteen years old and living in Kampala, the cutting sound of Nadya's dress, her walk (I had never before seen an Asian woman with such a strident walk), the excruciating anticipation of the dress tearing, made a much more ominous crackle than the fireworks display which had gone on a few months earlier, heralding in a new age as our pink masters took themselves and their Union Jacks home to Britain.

Nadya was eighteen and much too old to be in the school gym that day. The rest of us, all Asian, much younger, barely out of puff-sleeved dresses and cute socks, had just about started to dip our toes into the American graffiti era. A group of us, in a muddled sort of way, had started to dabble in teenage romance, surface gropes and wet kisses. Elvis and Cliff more or less told us what to do. Expressions like 'going steady' and '(not) all the way' had become part of the vocabulary. Guys started chewing gum and calling themselves names like 'Kid' and 'Fee'. The girls, discovering unsuspected depths of passion within, exploded like suddenly discovered oil in the back garden. I was sucked in by the ultra-cool 'Kid' and would have killed and died for him. I actually tried the latter one week when he was being excessively indifferent to my adoration, by taking five aspirins with coke which had been fizzed up – the combination, I had been told, was lethal. Many peculiar burps later life returned to normal, with him on a pedestal, and me at his feet.

This was one of the by-products of the arrival of romance into our lives. It made captives of the girls in a way that no arranged marriage had ever done. In the past, getting married was so beyond your control and so inevitable, you more or less expected to go through it, like inoculations, at some stage of your life. The negotiations were not in the gift of either the girl or the boy. You, therefore, did not waste your young life pining, imagining, and giving yourself over to courtship dreams and dramas.

The older generation of women in my life had a perfectly practical approach to the relationship between the sexes. They neither had nor demanded very much from men, except their basic functions of procreation, material provision and symbolic authority. None of these women dreamt of assigning to men responsibility for their own personal happiness, which they found through their children and the beautifully intricate relationships with other women relatives. They often had to suffer tough lives, but most managed to survive through resilience and self-reliance.

These women, including the stoics like my own mother and mother-in-law, whose lives make our pathetic little woes seem like nursery school knee grazes, look at us now and smile secretly at how little we are able to endure and how male indifference or faithlessness can break us. Yes, by the early sixties we were the first generation to become inmates of the seductive romance industry.

In some ways, therefore, the old structures in our strangely misplaced community had started to rattle, through the mimetic antics of this new brand of child for whom the roots in India had loosened and something else was needed to take their place. Before this time, even for our elder brothers and sisters the West had had very little real influence on social values.

East Africa had been under British rule since 1945. The 1948 census had shown about thirty-four thousand Asians and four thousand Europeans living in Uganda. The Asians had originally come in as indentured labourers to build the railways, and had then begun to take up the important buffer position between Blacks and whites as the commercial small-timers, the pettiest of petty bourgeoisie with a stake in the colonial status quo. They had conscientiously kept up with the rituals and values of the subcontinent (often in changed forms from the original, as these things do not travel well), pretending that they were really living just beyond the commuter belt of India.

Independence had been rather an unimpressive pop in Uganda, somewhat lacking the power and the glory one had come to expect from freedom struggles. But if one felt no great surges come out of the sea of change, you *did* feel a gentle rocking, subtle shifts of sand as when water laps around you when you are sitting at the edge of a deceptively sleepy sea, which isn't sleeping at all.

For these, in reality, were momentous times that just didn't feel the way momentous times should feel. We were on the threshold of enormous personal changes within the political upheavals that had accompanied decolonisation and those that were yet to come. We were not tangibly aware of this, although feelings of fear and freedom were about.

Everything was to change. The way we perceived Britain and the West; our lives as immigrant Asians; our politicisation, which was long overdue, and, most importantly, our view of Black Africans, as the imperative to acknowledge their humanity (and power) had become more than a moral necessity. Our survival depended on it. The pity was that ultimately so few of us understood this until it was too late. Everything in our lives was being redefined and all we could do with the unease initially was swirl around in the school gym.

The fifties in Uganda had been a time of eternal truths. The British, 'protecting' their protectorate, were there to stay. They were invincible and almost invisible. In Kenya, where the covetous ambitions of the white settlers were more obvious, the Mau Mau resistance had gouged out the god in the white man by showing how he could scare and squirm. Pan Africanism had grown in Tanzanian political circles. In Uganda, however, there was still a benign acceptance that the British were there to stay. Occasionally there was a perfunctory, lackadaisical protest, like the inept swipes one makes at unstoppable African flies when they brazenly cover your face in the midday sun. But beyond that we all padded about our business.

Asians were not the only people with a vested interest in the status quo. There were also the Baganda, the largest and most affluent tribe in southern Uganda, who felt some affinity with the British because of their own deep conservatism. They had, almost on first encounter with the early missionaries, espoused the Christian faith and much of what the whites had done was perfectly palatable to this adaptable and agreeable tribe. They certainly felt more safe with the British there than they did with some of the other Ugandan tribes. Their fears were borne out by history. Under the Amin and Obote regimes thousands of Bagandans were slaughtered.

That other rather less agreeable tribe, of whites, lived up on beautiful hilltops with dark green bushes wrapped around their bungalows. Impressively trained racist Alsatians foamed at every non-white who wandered past, naturally inquisitive to peer in through the opaque green wall. Most of the men were bureaucrats who swished past in cars, wearing khaki suits and expressionless faces. The population was small and unsettled, because here in Uganda, unlike Kenya, except for a small intelligentsia, they were only doing time for King and Country, and there really seemed no point in establishing even a nodding relationship with the Black and brown natives.

Their women shopped at two shops along the main road. Drapers, which was a miniscule nostalgic Liberty's, and Maison Michelle, where there were serious hats for sale. On the way to school I had been enthralled by a brown velvet one with innumerable folds. Looked at from one particular angle, it became the face of a ferocious bulldog. The sleek lady owner told me to push off because I was misting up her window.

There was a *de facto* apartheid system in operation which was understood by all. Nakasero school was a white school and the few white youngsters who were around were carefully and separately nurtured there. Somewhere half-way down the hills were placed affluent Asians with their schools and hospitals. And the poorer Asians lived downtown. All Asian children went to school. Few African children had the opportunity. When they did, it was literally under the trees with hardly any resources. The only exceptions were three church schools which were set up to produce a ruling Bagandan élite. Absurdly, these imitative bush Etons, which is what they tried to be, aimed to create in the young men and women with burning blazers on their backs, a sense of vanity and destiny.

England in the fifties and at the turn of the decade was full of contradictions. It was prohibitively inaccessible, yet it was, for so many of us, the only place to be, because it was so unbearably idyllic. Apples grew there, so did Christmas. Most of all, my heart watered at the thought of strawberries. (I remember reading a Noddy book in which Big Ears sliced a giant strawberry. I could feel the flesh of the fruit and the wee red droplets that jumped off the knife.)

Like paradise, the country was there, but there was no practical way of making travel arrangements to visit it. Anyway its magic lay in the emptiness of the longing. On the whole, the Africans had a much more cynical view of all this. They, after all, were not dispossessed.

The lust was most acutely felt by my generation and it was to grow as the decade proceeded. The older generation had felt a veneration for the mother country, and thought there was much to learn from those upright British men and women who had controlled the world at one time and won two world wars. They never wanted to belong to it, though.

The very rich Asians were different. They sent their children 'overseas' to get their further education, or in some situations even to snobbish boarding schools where the children would act out great fantasies that their fathers were sultans. These 'England returns' were the bane of our lives. They used to come home in August, carrying their baggage of snobbery to throw at us. The women wore fearsome long fingernails and nylon stockings in tropical temperatures. They were inevitably hairdressers or stenographers, a new word that created a new class of working Asian women. They arrogantly swept about for a few months, until marriages were arranged for them with suitable counterparts, 'England return' doctors or pharmacists, and they settled down ever after. These people did not challenge anything fundamental in the social structure. As in Japan today, theirs were merely masks, which it made good economic sense to put on. Marriages, for example, were still negotiated by families and sensible decisions reached, but now you invited a few Europeans, and had a wedding cake.

In one sense, this was not unusual in East Africa, where there had been an exciting synthesis of four powerful cultural influences, but no mixing. So the purity of the individual cultures – Arab, African, European, and Asian, had dissolved and each group had changed (the British proving to be most resistant, of course), but they had remained separate. Things were therefore fixed in their own way and who you revered and despised was immutable. As we moved into the pre-independence era, these immutables began to cave in. The African was no longer prepared to accept that working as a domestic servant fifteen hours a day, for five pounds a month, degradation thrown in, was part of her/his destiny. Small-scale individual revolts began to appear on the domestic front. My generation was no longer certain that we were prepared to go the way of our parents in these attitudes towards the Africans.

Other important changes had also occurred at the onset of the sixties through the historical processes of urbanisation and immigration, as a result of which African and Asian women assumed much more domestic power than they would ever have had in the African and Indian villages from which they originated. Pioneering experiences force down debilitating gender roles at a deep level. (Of course they appear again with a vengeance when the community settles down as in the United States.) Many seeds were thus sown in the fifties and the great harvests came in the sixties, because of what happened in Britain in that decade and what happened to East Africa.

In terms of our own lives too, these factors altered perceptions profoundly. If pop music is a harbinger of popular movements, when Elvis and Cliff first arrived into our lives, we were bowled over, but the impact was mostly superficial. Our parents objected to them in a desultory sort of way; there was no sense of threat at all. Our parents had far too much confidence in the enduring nature of their roots and the propriety of Britain. The fixed images of that country were that it was full of disciplined patriots, noble James Masons every one of them. ('The British', for me at the time, always conjured up a picture of a man of a certain age in uniform.)

Imagine their consternation, then, when the uprightness of whiteness cracked even in the pubescent days of the sixties. Our parents began to feel uneasy and threatened – first by the Beatles, then by the Rolling Stones. Nadya symbolised the change for me. Here was a woman, no stenographer, who would never pander to the whims of a male boss. She was a painter. She spoke of politics, of justice, peace and equality. She presented the emerging counter-culture of an England where the young were enshrining disorder and indiscipline as the brave new world. Where being British was suddenly not what it had always been cracked up to be.

The restlessness communicated itself to us initially as weakness, and held for us the same horror as children who discover their parents are not superhuman. What were we to make of Great Britain when her young (and it was the first time my image of Britain turned young) were rejecting that greatness, saying it was, as Bernard Levin describes in *The Pendulum Years*, 'too noisy, too ugly, too selfish, too unimaginative, too uncaring, too materialist, too majority oriented, too standardised in every way'?

Gradually, as the decade began to unfold, we began to think of ourselves in a strangely schizophrenic way. There were big thrills going on in Britain to which we wanted still to belong. And we did, wearing op-art dresses and ironing our hair profusely to get the look right. But the sexual freedom never came, because we rejected it. For the first time we felt in our heads a sense of moral superiority to the British. That amount of abandonment was wrong and we would have none of it. A real time for growing up that was. The rejection was selective, but the sense of Britain as an immoral force was to grow as the decade drew on and drugs and death began to sink into our lives, creating a panic we, as a community, had never felt before. Parents ordered their children to return home from Britain, which had become a dangerous place to be. Many refused and were lost forever.

Politically, Britain was also failing us as a community. We had thought we were so safe, that Britain would always care. When the crunch came, we had to cope with the blatant racism of the immigration legislation, and the treatment of Asians when they arrived in Britain.

By 1968, there were other movements that began to affect the national psyche of Uganda. The student riots and the Civil Rights movement, in separate and different ways, had demonstrated the power of group protests. While the latter added to the growth of Black pride in East Africa, the political leaders in Uganda were worried that similar student demonstrations in a young country like Uganda would create havoc. In an extraordinary gesture, President Obote and his wife invited fifty student leaders in the country to live with them in their beautiful state house for three months to find out and question how the government worked. I was there, and it was an unforgettable exercise in student participation which could never have happened in the West.

Disillusionment with the West grew as the years went on. How could we believe any more in a country which had produced the Profumo scandal, the drug culture, the Moors murders, etc., etc.?

For some of us Asians that realisation was a moment of liberation and we turned towards Uganda, the country that had nurtured us – we felt a need of and a commitment to it. The last years of the sixties produced the most exciting period I ever remember in Uganda. The university flourished. It was a truly international and multi-racial centre, where, for the first time, substantial numbers of white, Black and brown students committed to a new future gathered on the campus of Makerere University.

Everything mattered then. We were writing the first real history of Africa through African eyes. The literature department began to teach African, Indian, and Caribbean literature. In the schools a different kind of Brit began to arrive. To my secondary school came Mr Gregory, burning with passion for comprehensive education. He pulled down the walls partitioning the huts in which we studied, and started teaching creativity instead of English. He even flirted with us.

An Englishman showing a sexual interest in us was a completely unknown experience and we could barely cope with it. Mrs Bose, the very strict Indian maths teacher, who was sixty, was not pleased at this new brand of Englishman they had suddenly started to export from the good old country. He was corrupting her girls. When he decided to produce a spoof stage version of *The Avengers* as the annual school play, she nearly passed out.

But the sense of new beginnings and values, of feeling that the new world would step over the writhing body of the degenerating old world was a powerful one right across East Africa. For the first time people were arriving from America and Britain because we had something to teach them of the good life and not vice versa. The gross materialism of the sixties, the corruption of the West seemed a good thing not to have. Powerful writers, thinkers like Ali Mazrui were providing intellectual backup to the way we were feeling.

So in 1972, when I boarded a plane to Britain, my feelings were intensely confused. The childhood dreams were still there, they needed to come to fruition. I wanted desperately to see an orchard (I still haven't seen one), and be merry in Carnaby Street and buy bell-bottoms. Another part of me wanted to remain in Uganda, and grow with it and see the country become what the young of Britain were fighting for. We had a better chance, I felt, than you ever would. Yet the historical processes had made it impossible for that incipient relationship between Black and brown to grow. There were too few of us that were truly committed by then to an egalitarian society; to erase twenty-odd years of exploitation by our community. Equally, the sixties had taught me the most difficult lesson of all. That the land that had replaced India as my motherland was capable of betraying and destroying my humanity. That the laws and people of that country were working to keep me out after years of inviting me and seducing me to want to belong there. That hurt and still does.

But we came and saw. And some of the idealistic white children of the sixties became our friends and saw us often in a way that helped ease the hurt. They are the people who wanted to learn what we knew, wanted to eat what we cooked and were there when we needed them.

And the woman in me, as a child of the sixties, grew too. It became the free spirit that none of the women in my family had ever had a chance to be.

It happened because during that decade granite turned to water, the impossible became the perfectly do-able. Certainty vanished and with the ensuing dislocation came new beliefs that nothing should be as sacrosanct. And the principle of fluidity, not rigidity, became the moving force of my life.

Poems by
U. A. Fanthorpe

Love in a Cold Climate

AT AVERHAM

Here my four-year-old father opened a gate,
And cows meandered through into the wrong field.

I forgot who told me this. Not, I think,
My sometimes reticent father. Not much I know

About the childhood of that only child. Just
How to pronounce the name, sweetly deceitful

In its blunt spelling, and how Trent
Was his first river. Still here, but the church

Closed now, graveyard long-grassed,
No one to ask in the village. Somewhere here,

I suppose, I have a great-grandfather buried,
Of whom nothing is known but that, dying, he called

My father's mother from Kent to be forgiven.
She came, and was. And came again

To her sister, my great-aunt, for
Her dying pardon too. So my chatty mother,

But couldn't tell what needed so much forgiving,
Or such conclusive journeys to this place.

Your father, pampered only brother
Of many elder sisters, four miles away,

Grew up to scull on this river. My father,
Transplanted, grew up near poets and palaces,

Changed Trent for Thames. Water was in his blood;
In a dry part of Kent his telephone exchange

Was a river's name; he went down to die
Where Arun and Adur run out to sea.

Your father, going north, abandoned skiffs for cars,
And lived and died on the wind-blasted North Sea shore.

They might have met, two cherished children,
Among nurses and buttercups, by the still silver Trent,

But didn't. That other implacable river, war,
Trawled them both in its heady race

Into quick-march regiments. I don't suppose they met
On any front. They found our mothers instead.

So here I stand, where ignorance begins,
In the abandoned churchyard by the river,

And think of my father, his mother, her father,
Your father, and you. Two fathers who never met,

Two daughters who did. One boy went north, one south,
Like the start of an old tale. Confusions

Of memory rise: rowing, and rumours of war,
And war, and peace; the secret in-fighting

That is called marriage. And children, children,
Born by other rivers, streaming in other directions.

You like the sound of my father. He would
Have loved you plainly, for loving me.

Reconciliation is for the quick, quickly. There isn't enough
Love yet in the world for any to run to waste.

TITANIA TO BOTTOM

You had all the best lines. I
Was the butt, too immortal
To be taken seriously. I don't grudge you
That understated donkey dignity.
It belongs to your condition. Only,
Privately, you should know my passion
Wasn't the hallucination they imagined,
Meddling king and sniggering fairy.

You, Bottom, are what I love. That nose,
Supple, aware; that muzzle, planted out
With stiff, scratchable hairs; those ears,
Lofty as bulrushes, smelling of hay harvest,
Twitching to each subtle electric
Flutter of the brain! Oberon's loving
Was like eating myself – appropriate,
Tasteless, rather debilitating.

But holding you I held the whole
Perishable world, rainfall and nightjar,
Tides, excrement, dandelions, the first foot,
The last pint, high blood pressure, accident, prose.

The sad mechanical drone of enchantment
Finished my dream. I knew what was proper,
Reverted to fairyland's style.
                                    But Bottom, Bottom,
How I shook to the shuffle of your mortal heart.

CHAPLAINCY FELL WALK

There is always one out in front
With superior calves and experienced boots;

Always a final pair to be waited for,
Not saying much, pale, rather fat;

And the holy ones in the middle, making it
Their part to acclimatize the lonely and new,
Introducing cinquefoil, a heron, a view;

And a stout one who giggles, uniting us
In wonder at her unfaltering chokes;
But alarming too. For what is she laughing at?

And remote presence of hills;
And the absence of you.

LOOKING BACK

'. . . We're older than that now'

Angela Carter

Truly, It Felt Like
....
Year One
....

The sixties were the first, and may well turn out to be the only, time when we had an authentic intelligentsia in this country just like the ones in Europe and America – a full-blooded, enquiring rootless urban intelligentsia which didn't define itself as a class by what its parents had done for a living. And which earned its own living (to the extent that it *did* earn its living – a lot of us lived on the dole and thought, furiously, at our own pace) via ideas. It was an unusual historic moment; it was very exciting; I grew up in the fifties – that is, I was twenty in 1960, and, by God, I *deserved* what happened later on. It was tough, in the fifties. Girls wore white gloves.

I tend to blame a lot of what went on on the 1944 Education Act. Heavy irony, here. Blame? Well, some people seem to see the sixties, culminating in the summer of '68, as a giant aberration in the wonderfully tranquil and cohesive history of English social class; at least, that seems to be the current neo-Rightist revisionist line. So why not let a bit of soft liberal legislation carry the can. Nevertheless, the 1944 Education Act did indeed extend the benefits of further education to a select group of kids from working-class backgrounds, picked out *on account* of how they were extra-bright. Some of them were even permitted to go to Oxford and Cambridge. (Not me.) And were they grateful? Were they, hell. Did they say to themselves: 'God, if it hadn't been for the 1944 Education Act, I'd have gone the way of *Jude the Obscure*?' Never! We'd the full force of the Attlee administration behind us, too, and all that it stood for, that lingered on after the Tories got back in. All that free milk and orange juice and codliver oil made us big and strong and glossy-eyed and cocky and we simply took what was due to us whilst reserving the right to ask questions.

Besides, by the sixties, the 1944 Education Act had more or less percolated through the entire system, and the grammar schools themselves were on the point of turning into training camps for the class war since they were run by and for the children of the lower classes, by that time. (That was why Shirley Williams put a stop to them, of course; she couldn't stomach a situation like that.) They had to invent all those new universities, and the polytechnics, too, to cope with the pressure. In a country as brutally disfigured by class as Britain, an educational system based on some kind of working meritocracy offered some of the benefits of plastic surgery – a boost of the patient's self-confidence, for one thing.

Let me not get carried away by my own imagery.

We thought at the time we were 'classless', or had become 'classless', but, in fact, we were involved in the creation of this unprecedented and exponentially expanding intelligentsia. And we suddenly started getting on terribly well with the French and the Italians and the Germans, who'd been used to this sort of thing since the nineteenth century. Used, not to situations of social mobility as such, but used to situations of *intellectual* mobility. Try to imagine a French Orwell, it's very difficult; he was a kind of tourist in class terms, in a way that's quite incompatible with the whole idea behind a Popular Front. And, intellectually, Britain was opening itself up to Europe at all kinds of different levels – or so it seemed to me. Things were becoming accessible to me, in my early twenties, that I'd never imagined – ways of thinking, versions of the world, versions of history, of ways for societies to be.

I saw Godard's *Breathless* when it came out in 1959, and my whole experience of the next decade can be logged in relation to Godard's movies as if he were some sort of touchstone. I suppose all I was doing was going through some kind of intellectual apprenticeship of a generalised 'European' type, and I recognised and responded to a way of interpreting the world that suited my own instincts far more than the Leavisite version I was being given at university. (I went to university, to Bristol, in 1962, somewhat late, and studied English Lit.) The last words of *Weekend* – *fin du cinéma, fin du monde* – heavens! how they struck home!

Because towards the end of the sixties it started to feel like living on a demolition site – one felt one was living on the edge of the unimaginable; there was a constant sense of fear and excitement and, of course, it was to do with war.

Wars are great catalysts for social change and even though it was not specifically *our* war, the Vietnam war was a conflict between the First World and the Third World, between

211

Whites and Non-Whites and, increasingly, between the American people, or a statistically significant percentage thereof, and Yankee imperialism. And the people won, dammit. Whatever happened afterwards, however much they rewrite that war and whatever else the U.S. does, it was the first war in the history of the world where the boys were brought back from the front due to popular demand from their own side. But why should Britain have been so caught up in the consequences of U.S. foreign involvement? The more I think of it, the odder it seems . . . that so much seemed at stake in Vietnam, the very nature of our futures, perhaps. (It's considered sectarian eccentricity, or worse, to express similar concern these days about our very own ugly little colonial war in Northern Ireland.) On the positive side . . . an internationalism that wasn't in the least superficial. There was an extraordinary *camaraderie* amongst the rootless urban intelligentsia, and, no doubt, there always will be such a *camaraderie* although it's getting more and more difficult to stay rootless, what with the paucity of rented flats and the way they're cracking down on squats. (Of course, I've had a mortgage for years. That's middle age.)

So where does all the Swinging London stuff, pop music, hemlines, where did it all fit in? I'd like to be able to dismiss it all as superficial and irrelevant to what was really going on, people arguing about Hegel and so on, but I'm forced to admit there was a yeastiness in the air that was due to a great deal of unrestrained and irreverent frivolity. Do you remember a dreadful book by Richard Neville, *Play Power*? Tacky, tacky, tacky! But there's no denying that towards the end of the decade everyday life, even where I was living, in Bristol, took on the air of a continuous improvisation . . . the particularly leafy and graceful bit of Bristol where I lived attracted festal behaviour. *Carpe diem*. Pleasure. It didn't have to cost much, either.

One of the interesting things about the music boom – at least, I thought so at the time – was the way that young white kids from the most deprived parts of Britain, Liverpool, Newcastle, places not exactly sleek with prosperity in those days, although maybe compared to today . . . anyway, these poor whites took to the music of poor Blacks from the most wretchedly segregated and oppressed parts of the deep South of the U.S. like ducks to water. There was also that manifest display of sexuality – males for sale. Do you remember a novel that briefly best-sold around the turn of the decade, *Groupie*, it was called, I forget the name of the girl who wrote it. It was about the theory and practice of collecting fucks from pop singers in a manner that a less physically energetic age might have collected autographs. I suspect that manners had not been so liberal and expressive since the Regency – or maybe even since the Restoration, with the absence of syphilis compensated for in the mortality stakes by the arrival of hard drugs. (There has never been a period in human history where one has been able to eat one's cake and have it, alas.)

But the relaxation of manners, the sense of intellectual excitement, even the way, oh, God, you didn't have to shave your *armpits*. . . hemlines, politics, music, movies, everything both central and peripheral to my life was placed in the context of things I took absolutely for granted. For instance, the inevitability of the Labour government; over and above that, the absolute inevitability and permanence of the Welfare State. Do you remember the Claimants' Union? (Does it still exist?) It had a slogan: 'Bite the hand that feeds you.' Can you imagine any sane person approaching what's left of the social services in that spirit today? As if the person-in-the-street had the *right* to enough, or even to too much?

That's one of Blake's proverbs of 'Proverbs of Hell' – 'Enough. Or, too much.' Blake was the great poet of the times. 'The tigers of wrath are wiser than the horses of instruction.' That was on a wall in Notting Hill, as I recall. There was another piece of graffiti that troubled me a lot, all it said was: 'Chopped Pork'. But that was in the early seventies, when the graffiti had passed through its romantically apocalyptic phase and the hard-edge Situationalists were at it.

I was married most of the sixties – the sense of living on a demolition site was perfectly real, in one way, because we stopped being married in 1969. By which time the sexual revolution the papers were always going on about was more or less completed. I find it very odd that women who are otherwise perfectly sensible say that the 'sexual revolution' of the sixties only succeeded in putting more women on the sexual market for the pleasure of men. What an odd way of looking at it. This seems to deny the possibility of sexual pleasure to women except in situations where it's so hedged around with qualifications that you might as well say, like my mother used to say, 'Don't do it until you've got the ring on your finger.'

But certainly the introduction of more or less 100 per cent effective methods of birth control, combined with the relaxation of manners that may have derived from this technological innovation or else came from God knows where, changed, well, everything. Sexual pleasure was suddenly divorced from not only reproduction but also status, security, all the foul traps men lay for women in order to trap them into permanent relationships. Sex as a medium of pleasure. Perhaps pleasure is the wrong word. More like sex as an expression of is-ness. Of course, the British are traditionally very tight-lipped about sex and Americans even more so – indeed, full of repressed Protestant fear and loathing, in my experience. So it isn't surprising there has been such a backlash, especially within the women's movement.

But then, again, there's no such thing as a pure pleasure and if the relations between men and women were simplified, in some ways, by changes in sexual behaviour – at least you didn't have to marry somebody – then in other ways they became much, much more complex. Women tend to be raised with a monolithic notion of 'maleness', just as men are raised with the idea of a single and undifferentiated femininity. Stereotyping. *Real* men, especially when approached by women acting in ways they're not supposed to act, can behave like fifteen-year-old girls in the photostory magazines. This can come as a shock.

It turns out that human relations are very complex and often very painful regardless at what moment during their course sexual intercourse takes place. It seems strange this insight should be so newsworthy, or should be used to try to put the sexual clock back to the tortuous repression I recall from my teenage years.

It is the sex that people are really thinking of when they talk about the inexpressible decadence of the sixties. (And it wasn't just heterosex, either; oh, dear, no.) And the entire spree was sustained by a buoyant economy; everybody was so very, very rich, you see, due to sponging off the state or, I don't know, cornering the market in tie-dyed underpants or cover versions of aged Mississippi blues singers or patchouli-scented candles. Or. But at that time Britain was a low rent, cheap food country with relatively low wages and high taxes – most people I knew lived on very, very little. We were early into recycling – second-hand furniture, old houses, old clothes were dirt cheap in the sixties, or else free. You could strip a derelict house, nobody else wanted the stuff. Oh, God, those vast, whitewashed rooms with bare-board floors and a mattress in a corner with an Indian coverlet on it . . . when will *World of Interiors* resurrect it, the pure asceticism of the late sixties?

In those days, you could afford London Transport even if you were on the dole. That must have been where the taxes went. 'If the fool persist in his folly, he becomes wise.' I suppose that was how I came to feminism, in the end, because still and all there remained something out of joint and it turned out that was it, rather an important thing, that all the time I thought things were going so well I was in reality a second-class citizen. But that particular proverb of hell was another of the mottoes of the decade – it was the time of the loony. I suppose that R. D. Laing's *The Divided Self* was one of the most influential books of the sixties – it made madness, alienation, hating your parents . . . it made it all glamorous. God knows what he did for people who were *really* mad, apart from making them feel smug and richly self-righteous, but he certainly set the pace for that crazy hinge of the decade, from 1968 on – things started to calm down after the U.S. withdrew from Vietnam. And there was an extraordinarily lugubrious movie by Bergman, *Persona*, that a lot of people said caught the spirit of the times. (It didn't for me; I stuck with *Weekend*.) That was Laingian, too.

All the cases Laing discusses in *The Divided Self* predate publication by some years. Either in *The Divided Self* or in the other book, the name of which I forget, Laing talks about the eccentric dress of a young patient – the boy arrives wearing a sort of frock coat, looking like Kierkegaard. Laing is very struck by it. By 1965, there would have been nothing eccentric-looking about this young man at all. He probably wouldn't have bothered with psychiatry by then, either. He'd have persisted in his folly. He'd have founded a sect.

Gaynor Griffiths
and Mildred Lee

Marilyn Monroe versus
the Hippies

Think of someone with streaky, long hair wearing 'psyche-delic' flary bell-bottomed trousers causing havoc and pro-testing about the prices at a local shopping centre, or any other excuse for a Saturday afternoon 'demo'. They were the rebels, they had the foot-wiping hair, the uncared-for com-plexion, the flower power, flares, drugs, and 'All you need is lurve'. They were the Hippies. They are the centre of mockery for the teenagers of the eighties.

Think of a perfect set of teeth behind a perfect pair of perfectly painted red lips, set on a perfect, spot-free snow-white complexion, topped with a perfect crown of white-blonde curls, the type of girl most of us envy, who's popular with all the boys and has the type of figure that we all dream of. She has all the clothes you want and the beauty of an angel. She is Marilyn.

Think of us, the eighties, clean-cut, and worried by appearance. Our dull unoriginal life-style and uninteresting media blurred by dreams of luxuries, fast cars and hi-fi systems. What are Molly Ringwald, Michael J. Fox and Tom Cruise compared with the all-time greats, Elvis Presley, James Dean, Doris Day and Marilyn Monroe?

Rock 'n' roll, the larger the quiff the better, under-laced flary skirt, red lips, baseball jackets, caps, mitts, etc . . . Sound familiar? Yes, they are from the fifties, and now the eighties too. We have mentioned the fact that our media today is boring but the fashions of today can't even be original. But we are not complaining, we enjoy this sexy past that our clothes have come from, but we add to it with the masculinity of today, e.g. Doc Martens.

What we are trying to get across is that Marilyn Monroe was a fifties hit and now that fifties fashions are 'in' so are the things that came with the fifties: Marilyn, *Grease*, rock 'n' roll and the music. The sixties fashions are *not* 'in', as we consider PVC a cheap and ugly form of clothing.

In the sixties women wore 'the Victoria and Albert Museum' look, unbelievably short skirts (known as 'buttock cutters') that showed their cheap paper knickers to the world; they also wore thigh-high boots (beetle crushers) that had cork platforms as long and wide as their skirts. Men, however chose the 'loud' look as their psychedelic flares clashed with their floral kipper ties in pink and orange shirts. Major hairstyles consisted of the 'easy come easy go' look of the unwashed/unbrushed thatch of straggly hair or the alternative 'cared for' look – hours of painful back combing to form the 'beehive', or hours of expensive cutting to get the geometry-set plastic appearance. The make-up of the time consisted of a sludgy 'drugged out' look of black circled eyes and white or slimey coloured lipstick. Music was of the same texture; for example it always sounds as though it was being played at the wrong speed. Basically hippies were filthy, didn't believe in covering body odours and a hair brush was unheard of.

Jackie, Blue Jeans and 'I want to be loved by you'. What have they got in common? Romance. A boyfriendless girl, a girlfriendless boy, they both want it, most teenagers do. So now what is the difference between 'Diamonds are a girl's best friend' and 'We shall not be moved'? If you say one's romantic and the other is not you would be correct. If you were a 'Lonely Heart' which would you prefer? The Marilyn Monroe one. The point we are trying to explain here is that Marilyn knows what we're about, her films and songs explain this. Hippies are rough, they sleep outside and believe everything is 'Heavy, Man'.

The press only supply what the readers want to read and will go out of their way to get it. Many people at that time didn't really like the hippies and were probably frightened of them, so the press wrote some terrible and probably untrue things about the hippies, thus giving them a bad name. On the other hand men were swooning over Marilyn and women adored her beauty even though many were very envious, so the press wrote good things about her – hoping to win the readers' approval – thus giving Marilyn a good name, so propaganda did have quite a lot to do with the public's opinion.

Our parents try and tell us good things about the sixties but we think they are fooling themselves. They say that women's liberation was started then, but we know that it was started by Emmeline Pankhurst and those women long, long before. They say that Peace stuff started then, but they had ban-the-bomb in the fifties. If they are right that ecology started in the sixties that is one good thing, and so is having contraception, and the law letting you be gay, but it isn't much. In the fifties there was real style and in the seventies there was feminism, and politics, and us. The sixties were a mess.

Mocking one's parents about their past – teenagers' favourite pastime. Well, if you were an upwardly mobile trendy would you like to admit the hippies we described above were your parents: they're good for stealing shirts and jackets off, for cooking your meal and for writing your sick note for PE but when it comes to style you just have to laugh. The sixties were the time of our parents' prime therefore to not laugh and mock at that time would be telling your parents they were correct. That would never do!

219

Biographies
●●●●●●●●●●●●●●●●●●

Gina Adamou: 'I was born in Nicosia, Cyprus in 1945 and came to Britain with my family in 1960. I now live with my husband in Haringey. Two of my children are at university and the other at college. I am working at the moment as a self-employed retailer of women's coats. I am active in the Labour Party and now seeking election as a borough councillor.

My other interests include music and books. My favourite songs from the sixties are Elvis' "Are you lonesome tonight?" and "It's now or never".'

Yasmin Alibhai: 'I was born in Uganda and lived there until 1972. After getting a degree in Literature at Makerere University, I came to England and did an M.Phil at Oxford. Since training as a radio journalist I have worked both for Radio 4 ("Woman's Hour") and the World Service and have also published in the *Guardian, City Limits* and *New Society*. I was also once a senior lecturer in Equal Opportunities for ILEA. Now I am working as the editor of "Race and Society", for *New Society* and live in London with my beautiful son.'

Leila Berg: 'I was born and grew up in Salford, then lived for fifty years in various parts of London, but have made a move recently, to East Anglia. I have one son, one daughter and four grandchildren. I wrote for the *Guardian* during the sixties and have also written many books for children; in 1973 I won the Eleanor Farjeon Award for services to children's literature. My favourite song from the sixties? Can't do that. All the songs of Bob Dylan, Judy Collins, Joan Baez, Buffy Sainte-Marie; many of Leonard Cohen's; and Josh White singing "Wanderings"; Billie Holiday singing "God Bless the Child", "I Love My Man", "The Sunny Side of the Street", and "As Time Goes By"; Marlene Dietrich singing "Stay 'way from My Window"; the Spinners singing "The Leaving of Liverpool"; Ewan McColl singing "Dirty Old Town"; The Goons singing "I'm Walking Backwards for Christmas" and – for very personal reasons – Marion Anderson's recording of "All our Trials, Lord" and Ella Fitzgerald's "But Not For Me".'

Angela Carter was born in 1940 and lives in South London. She is a writer; her last book was a collection of short stories, *Black Venus* (1985). She edited the anthology *Wayward Girls and Wicked Women* for Virago in 1986. She could not think of one single song to call her favourite.

Barbara Castle is now Labour Member of the European Parliament for Greater Manchester. She was born in 1910, and was Labour MP for Blackburn from 1945–1979. She was a Cabinet Minister, with various portfolios – overseas development, transport, employment and productivity, and social services – throughout the Labour Party governments of the sixties and seventies, and has published two volumes of diaries covering these administrations. She now lives near High Wycombe.

Julie Christie is now, as she was throughout the sixties, an actress. She was born in India in 1940, and after going to the Central School of Speech and Drama, began her film career in *Crooks Anonymous* in 1962. She won the Best Actress Oscar for her role in *Darling* in 1964 and also starred in *Billy Liar*

(1963), *Dr Zhivago* (1965), *Far from the Madding Crowd* (1966), and numerous other films through the seventies and eighties. She now lives in London.

Susan Dowell: 'I was born in the late summer of 1942 and grew up in suburban Twickenham, next door to the rugby ground. I returned to London after Africa, in 1970, where my husband became Chaplain to the London School of Economics. We took over a derelict house which we made into a student hostel. Here I worked with children again – helping to set up a day nursery – had two more (twins) myself, realised I'd always been a feminist and thanked God for the movement.

'Since 1976, I've been involved with the Peace Movement's Christian wing, working for five years with Pax Christi (Roman Catholic) and now mostly with Christian CND. We moved to the Welsh border a year ago where there is more time for peace activism and for my writing.

'"Moon River" (from *Breakfast at Tiffany's*) was my favourite song – Holly Golightly's song.'

U.A. Fanthorpe: 'Born 1929, educated perfunctorily in Surrey and began to learn at Oxford (St Anne's College). After sixteen years teaching I decided I wanted to learn more about myself and the world, and found a job as clerk/ receptionist in a small neurological hospital in Bristol. I'd always meant to write, but teaching interfered, whereas low grade hospital work pitched me into poetry. Three books published so far by Harry Chambers/Peterloo Poets, and a fourth due out this year, also a third volume of poetry for children (Oxford University Press), and a selection from the three Peterloo collections was published in 1986 as a King Penguin. (The others in the series are all men . . .) I live in Gloucestershire with the woman who has shared my life for the last twenty-one years.'

Joan Fletcher was born in Wales in 1949, but has lived in London since 1968. She has two children and works in a wine bar in the City. She is married. Her favourite song from the sixties is 'A Whiter Shade of Pale' by Procol Harum; she still keeps the record lovingly.

222

Gaynor Griffiths and Mildred Lee: 'All our efforts to write a decent biography have been thwarted by the editor (my mother, unfortunately – *Mildred*) who says we are being either too silly or too boring. We were born in 1972 (Gaynor) and 1973 (Mildred) – one of us lives in a vicarage underneath a tower block and the other lives in a tower block over a vicarage – both in East London. We are planning to be very rich and very famous when we grow up – in the meantime we both go to (different) girls-only (worse luck) comprehensive schools.'

'Jane': 'I was born in 1938. I divorced Tom in 1970 and now live with my second husband, a solicitor, and our son near Portsmouth. I cannot remember any popular songs from the '60s and think that was either because I was too old or because the decade passed in such a blur for me.'

Lee Kane: 'I was born in 1944; my father was African from South Africa, and my mother was Scots. I was brought up in post-war Britain and was sixteen at the beginning of the sixties. Married and later a single parent, I was not an active participant in the sixties "revolution" although my subsequent actions were profoundly affected by those events. In the seventies I was involved in a number of activities connected with Black people and Black women's rights. I am currently a student of African History, but have also worked as a social worker and legal adviser.'

Sheila MacLeod: 'I was born in the Isle of Lewis, Scotland, but have lived mainly in the south of England. Started writing (for publication) when a student at Somerville College, Oxford, where I read English. I am the author of seven novels, the latest of which is *Axioms* (Quartet); *The Art of Starvation*, an analytical/autobiographical account of anorexia nervosa (Virago); and *Lawrence's Men and Women* an examination of male and female characters in the fiction of D.H. Lawrence (Heinemann). I have also written two TV plays and a considerable amount of journalism, and have taught creative writing at various venues, including the Arvon Foundation, the City Lit and Antioch University. Now I live mainly in

London but tend to sneak off to a Breton hideaway at every possible opportunity.

A favourite song is rather more difficult, because so many from that period have such intimate associations. But I do remember that, at the time, Procul Harum's '"A Whiter Shade of Pale"' seemed to sum up that rather spaced-out, floating sense of freedom in which all things were possible. I first heard it driving along in an open car with my friend Chelita (whose husband was Tony Secundna, Procul Harum's manager at the time) past the hideous town of High Wycombe, where I had been so unhappy at school, and feeling one of those rare sensations of being blissfully joyful – and aware of it.'

Anne McDermid was born in Wales and spent much of her childhood in the United States and Canada. 'I graduated from Victoria College, University of Toronto, and then went wandering in search of excitement for several years which included the Parisian adventure. In between throwing stones at policemen, I earned a living by translating sleazy American detective novels into French. I happened to drop into London for a brief spell on my way to somewhere else and accidently fell into being a literary agent. I am still here.'

Sara Maitland: 'I was born in London in 1950 and brought up there and in south-west Scotland. My mother once snapped the television off while the Animals were singing "House of the Rising Sun" because she thought Eric Clapton's sweating was obscene. This made it the first sixties song I ever took any notice of and on those grounds offer it as my favourite (see Introduction). After such an unpromising start I have gone on to become a feminist, a mother, a vicar's wife and a writer. My most recent fiction is a collection of short stories, *Telling Tales*, and *Arky Types*, a novel co-written with Michelene Wandor. For Virago I have, with Jo Garcia, co-edited another collection, *Walking on the Water*, and also written *Vesta Tilley*, a Virago Pioneer. I live in the East End of London.'

Frances Molloy was born in Derry, Northern Ireland, in 1947. 'After a patchy education I left school at fifteen to work in a local pyjama factory. In 1965 I spent a short time as a nun. In 1970 I decided to "emigrate" to England; I now live in County Sligo. I started writing in 1980 and my first novel *No Mate for the Magpie* (from which my contribution to this book is taken) was published by Virago in 1985.'

Moureen Nolan and Roma Singleton are sisters. They were born and raised in the West Derby area of Liverpool. Moureen was educated at Notre Dame Convent Grammar School, Mount Pleasant. She is thirty-four, married with two children and teaches English at a secondary school in Widnes where she now lives. Her favourite song from the sixties is 'Waterloo Sunset' by the Kinks. Her ambition is to ghost write the autobiography of someone famous.

Roma attended and was expelled from the same Catholic Grammar school. She now teaches behaviourally disturbed boys at a special school in Liverpool. She is thirty-eight, single and also lives in Widnes. Her ambition is to retire to the safety of running her own dog kennels. Favourite song from the sixties? Easy – 'Penny Lane'.

Sue O'Sullivan was born in 1940 and now lives in London and works for Sheba Feminist Publishers and the *Pink Paper*. She enjoys having grown-up children. Her favourite sixties group is the Everly Brothers, and her favourite song was called 'Duke of Earl' – although she cannot now remember who sang it.

Alexandra Pringle: 'As expected, I failed to get into university and ended up at Cambridge Tech, which was the beginning of Life for me. I went on to teach English in Florence, returning a year later to seek my fortune. Then followed a period as editorial assistant on a small art magazine, *Art Monthly*. This gave me an intense interest in artists, racing cyclists and partying in The Plough, Museum Street, the Tin Pan Alley Club and the French Pub. I joined Virago in 1978 as a twenty-five-year-old slave, and am still here, now as a thirty-five-year-old editorial director. I am married to the art critic Tim Hilton. We have a small son and a lot of abstract paintings. I have deserted Chelsea for Hampstead. The only things I miss about the sixties are Biba and the Beatles. What I enjoy about the eighties is being grown-up and doing what I like.'

Terri Quaye: 'Born 1940 into a family from Ghana, Barbados and England, I began life among the blitz in London's dockland. Earliest memories are my parent's rehearsals, shows, dressing rooms. By early teens I was singing regularly in jazz clubs. From the '60s I performed internationally as a jazz singer, working with many of the world's leading American jazz musicians. While this career reflected my love and need of music, my work as a percussionist evolved from the necessity to both assert and edify my roots in order to live in Britain. During the 1970s, I ran children's Black Music workshops in Brixton's Dark & Light Theatre and introduced Black cultural studies at Latchmere House Remand Centre for teenage offenders. Taught Europe's first Women's percussion workshops at London's Women's Art Alliance, and formed 'MoonSpirit' – England's first all-women jazz group. In 1982 I moved to Washington D.C. as Artist-in-Residence at the National Museum of African Art, Smithsonian Institution, lecturing and performing throughout the USA, and returned in 1985 to establish the Black Music Archives. Now in my late forties, I'm completing an Mmus. degree in Ethnomusicology. Compositions include scores for 'In Exile with An African Head', 'Care and Control', 'Patterns' (UK) and 'Return of the Kitchen Sisters' (USA). As a photographer 'Music – A Way of Life' (London, 1986), 'Black Edge' (Mappin Art Gallery 1987), 'Pacific, Music – Ancient & Modern' (Commonwealth Institute 1988).

Marsha Rowe: 'I left Sydney, Australia, when I was twenty-three. I then lived in London for seven years. After leaving *Spare Rib* magazine which I co-founded, I moved to Yorkshire. I had a daughter in 1980. In 1983 I returned to London. Motherhood and moving, loving and coping have taken up much of my time since then. I've worked as a freelance writer, proof-reader, editor, astrologist, and I now work as editor at Serpent's Tail Publishing. My favourite song of the sixties: Aretha Franklin singing Sam Cook's "A change is gonna come".'

Patricia Vereker: 'I was born in north London in 1920. I was educated at North London Collegiate College when it was in Camden Town and at University College, London. I married a university teacher and we have three children, a son and two daughters (in that order). I have taught part-time in various colleges and departments of education. I am now a part-time "voluntary lady". I have served as a magistrate for the past twenty-five years in Liverpool, Durham and now Oxford. I am a member of the Oxfordshire Area Probation Committee and I also chair a voluntary committee which manages "bed sit" accommodation for ex-offenders in co-operation with the Probation Service. We are at present trying to set up a new scheme to support "difficult to place" mentally disordered people in the community, many of whom are ex-offenders. Apart from this, I rejoice in my grandchildren, for whom I have no responsibility.'

Michelene Wandor is a poet, playwright, critic and short story writer. Her poetry includes *Upbeat, Gardens of Eden*; her short stories include *Guests in the Body*, and various anthologies; her critical work on theatre includes *Carry on, Understudies* (on theatre and sexual politics), *Look Back in Gender* (on the family and sexuality in post-war British drama). Her prolific work for the radio includes an eight-part dramatisation of *The Brothers Karamazov* and the film of *The Belle of Amherst*, which she adapted for Thames TV from William Luce's play about Emily Dickinson, and which won an international Emmy Award in 1987.